Contents

Acknowledgements

The author and publishers would like to thank Mike Dowden, Jackie Pfister and Kathy Scruton for their invaluable comments on the draft manuscript; and Amanda Molcher and the staff and pupils of Heronsgate School, Milton Keynes for being such enthusiastic participants in the photo sessions for this book.

We are also grateful to The Watts Publishing Group/Orchard Books for permission to reproduce extracts from *A Bun for Barney* by Joyce Dunbar.

ENGLISH

SPEAKING & LISTENING

FOR THE REVISED NATIONAL CURRICULUM

KS KEY STRATEGIES

Gordon Lamont

JOHN MURRAY

Other titles in the **Key Strategies** series:

Planning Primary Science, Revised National Curriculum Edition by Roy Richardson, Phillip Coote and Alan Wood
Primary Science: A Complete Reference Guide by Michael Evans
Physical Education: A Practical Guide by Elizabeth Robertson
From Talking to Handwriting by Daphne M Tasker
Helping with Handwriting by Rosemary Sassoon
Planning Primary Geography by Maureen Weldon and Roy Richardson
Planning Primary History by Tim Lomas, Christine Burke, Dave Cordingley, Karen McKenzie and Lesley Tyreman
Music: A Practical Guide for Teachers by Alan Biddle and Lynn Dolby

First published in 1995 by
John Murray (Publishers) Ltd
50 Albemarle Street, London W1X 4BD

Photography by Chris Fairclough

Illustrations by Chris Mutter

Layouts by Martin Adams

Typeset by Anneset, Weston-super-Mare

Printed in Great Britain by St Edmundsbury Press, Bury St Edmunds

A CIP catalogue record for this book is available from the British Library

ISBN 0-7195-7020-4

INTRODUCTION

Introduction

The importance of Speaking and Listening

The first words spoken on the surface of the moon are famous. So famous that we are sure we can leave you to fill in the word bubble yourself. These first words were not useful, practical, descriptive or scientific. They were of no consequence to the moon landing mission. Yet at the time there was much speculation about what those first words would be. Why did they seem so important? Part of the answer lies in the media's need for a 'sound bite' – preferably an endlessly quotable one-liner. But behind that lies the value and status that we attach to speech.

We believe spoken language to be one of the most significant defining features of humankind. We may use our pens and word processors regularly, but it is our voices which most reveal what we are to the world – with their subtlety of interaction, delicate play of expression, range of tonal qualities and myriad uses from the mundane to the profane, from words of ecstasy to expressions of the deepest despair. We use our voices calmly, angrily and to express every kind of thought and feeling. We use them to buy groceries and to propose marriage, to communicate with babies and to mark the end of life. And you, as a teacher, use your voice and listen to your children's voices throughout the day.

Learning to use spoken language effectively and to listen intelligently are amongst the most life-enhancing skills that any teacher can pass on. Yet this is not always appreciated. However eagerly a baby's first words are awaited, and however great the reward for those precious first words, parental and adult enthusiasm for children's spoken language diminishes over time. Verbal development is taken for granted. By the time a child goes to school there is little reward for using a new word or explaining a complex idea. Most adult reward and enthusiasm is reserved for the written word, correct spelling, neat handwriting or a cleverly written story.

One aim of English AT1, and of the suggested activities in this book, is to redress this imbalance, giving verbal development and listening skills the status and value which they deserve both in the school and in the home. This book recognises and celebrates the prime importance of speaking and listening in children's personal development.

Speaking and listening are skills essential to our children's development and, as the Kingman Report (April 1988) most powerfully argued, improving these skills gives them more power over their own lives.

Assisting children's learning across the curriculum

Most of us learn best through talk. The more complex the skills being learned the more important it is to talk about them, to make them our own and to discuss problems which arise. It is equally important to develop listening skills, the ability to make mental notes and to listen purposefully. This applies at any age and across the curriculum.

We realise that speaking and listening are useful skills for such subjects as English and Drama, but even a carefully worded scientific paper is invariably the outcome of a long process of experimentation, verbal explanation of ideas and discussion. This process leads to a gradual clarification of ideas.

> Year 1 children are working in pairs on their first scientific enquiry, trying to determine which of a number of objects will sink or float. As they work, they use language to describe physical objects and events, to predict outcomes and to report back verbally on the results, gradually developing a shared vocabulary to describe accurately what is happening. (See Sink or Float, p.56.)

Enriching children's thinking and writing

The link between thinking, speaking and writing is well known. Clarity and precision in one leads to clarity and precision in the others; effective speaking, for example, contributes to effective writing. A richness of spoken language, a range and subtlety of speech, and a command of different registers from standard English to colloquial conversation, will all be of benefit to children's writing. Developing verbal communication also develops the inner person – we think as we speak and a richly expressed life has its corollary in a rich inner experience.

> Both classes are working together on a 'Dragon' poem. The children are thinking up words relating to dragons, forming pictures in their minds and stretching their vocabulary to find words to evoke feelings, smells and sounds. Finally they perform their 'Dragon' poem. The process has involved the whole school in exploring a scene through language, thereby extending children's written and spoken communication. (See Dragons, p.39.)

Tackling social and emotional issues

A class which can discuss problems such as bullying, theft, and name-calling can acknowledge emotion and learn to deal with it. A class which can face up to difficulties together through discussion, acting in role, talking in groups, etc. will be well equipped to learn together and to face up to life's dilemmas as individuals. How many of the social problems which children face later in life would be less acute if they had learnt to listen before talking and to talk before acting?

> A mixed class of Year 5/6 children is using Forum Theatre to examine dilemmas in a safe, protected environment. Two children are enacting a difficult confrontation with a stranger. The teacher is pleased with the depth of understanding that they are displaying. (See Saying 'No', p.139.)

Developing children's own attitudes, values and opinions

Most of us (adults and children) try out our new attitudes, values and opinions by talking about them. We may use the context of an informal discussion with a friend or a more formal situation such as an encounter group or workplace meeting. Since we naturally use speech to express and explore our opinions, speech is a powerful means of introducing children to new ideas, and of getting them to consider their own response to opposing viewpoints.

A Year 5 class is engaging in an ecology debate. A proposal for a new road in the area has become a live issue, with local people and children in the school lining up on both sides of the argument. The school has used the opportunity to run a formal debate in which the opposing viewpoints are expressed, heard and considered. (See Ecology, p.153.)

Preparing children for adult life and the world of work

Although a well-crafted letter of application may secure an interview it is the person who can best convey his or her talents and respond intelligently in an interview who will be offered the job.

Perhaps more important, as it is a core skill for adult life, is the ability to participate in small group discussions, to offer ideas and to listen effectively. Small groups form the basis for so much learning, training, planning and decision making. A child who can develop and use these qualities in school will be more readily listened to and appreciated.

A Year 6 class is preparing to present the findings of their Playground Survey. Together they have agreed on and designed a questionnaire, conducted interviews and reported back on their findings. They have considered the most appropriate means of conveying their findings to the rest of the class. Now they have the challenging task of making a presentation. (See Design a Playground, p.166.)

Encouraging creative expression

Speaking and listening skills are important for participation in or appreciation of theatre, music, performed poetry, opera, radio and television. They are also the life blood of any co-operative arts venture.

Year 3 children are creating their own performance of a puppet play. They have negotiated and planned together, considered the basic features of the genre and used them to best effect to give their performances impact. The class work results in five performances of varying quality and a new dynamic that comes from working creatively together and learning to use a new medium. (See Hanuman, p.113.)

For all these reasons, and for the overarching importance of developing each child's full, human potential, this book aims to offer practical suggestions for furthering speaking and listening in the school environment.

Creating a school policy for Speaking and Listening

If you have already written half-a-dozen policy documents in the past year you might feel that there is nothing to writing this one. Speaking and Listening is, however, an unusual animal within the school curriculum and so, rather than fast-forwarding you to a sample policy, we feel that it would be more appropriate to tease out the process of creating one. The following situation describes a fictitious, but possible, departmental INSET day.

INSET day

The cast

June Cox: The Head
Mrs Cooper: Receptionist
Mrs Marsh: Y1
Mrs Andoh: Y2 and
   Language co-ordinator
Mrs Bales: Y3

Mr Hughes: Y4
Mrs Wise: Y5
Mr Bennett: Y6, INSET cynic
Julie Phillips: neighbouring Head
Mr Gummer: the (absent) INSET
   leader

7.45 am
Imagine the Head of Murrayville Primary School.
She's in her office – with a cup of coffee rapidly cooling on the bookshelf, trying to finish a whole day's admin before nine o'clock because today is an INSET day, a day of working and learning together with her staff, with the focus on 'Speaking and Listening'. She's booked an excellent trainer. She's been told he's brilliant, if unorthodox. Should be a stimulating day. But till then there's . . .

7.55 am

The phone rings. It's the trainer she'd booked three months ago – or actually it's his teenage son.

'My Dad asked me to phone. He can't come today. He's got a sore throat. He can't speak. He says he hopes that the notes he sent last week will be useful.'

The suspicious sick note brought in once a week by Karen Stacey flashes into her mind: 'My Mum kept me at home because I had lost my voice . . . '. *Do I believe him? Or has he just got a hangover?*

She allows herself a second or two to recover then gazes at the trainer's notes. Phrases like 'entitlement to personal language sphere' and 'rubric of appropriate vocal registers' float before her eyes. Of course she didn't take any notice at the time. What does all this stuff mean?

Cancel the meeting? Can't.

Change to a safer topic? Can. But that would be chickening out.

Go for it? Yes.

8.00 am
Time to push away the event leader's material (and him with it) and get on with some rapid planning. It'll be basic and down to earth because it has to be. It'll use resources that are close to hand because there are no others.

Today's admin can wait till tonight. Deep breath . . . Right.

Fifty minutes later she has a plan. (See Figure 0.1 below.)

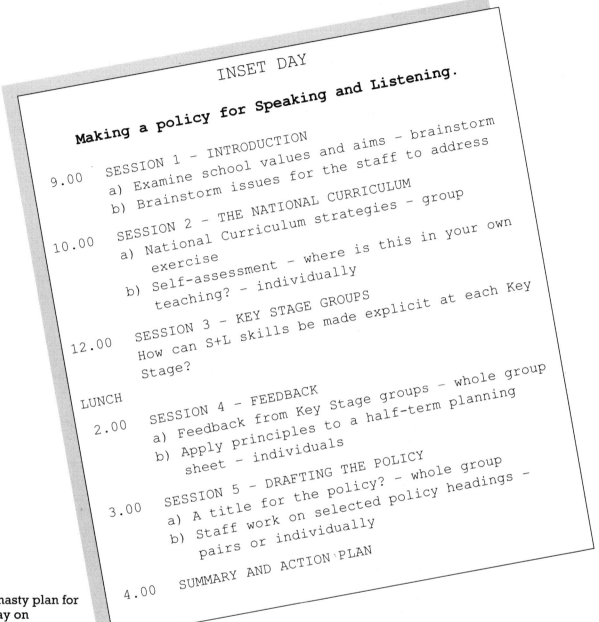

INSET DAY

Making a policy for Speaking and Listening.

9.00   SESSION 1 – INTRODUCTION
        a) Examine school values and aims – brainstorm
        b) Brainstorm issues for the staff to address

10.00   SESSION 2 – THE NATIONAL CURRICULUM
        a) National Curriculum strategies – group
           exercise
        b) Self-assessment – where is this in your own
           teaching? – individually

12.00   SESSION 3 – KEY STAGE GROUPS
        How can S+L skills be made explicit at each Key
        Stage?

LUNCH

2.00   SESSION 4 – FEEDBACK
        a) Feedback from Key Stage groups – whole group
        b) Apply principles to a half-term planning
           sheet – individuals

3.00   SESSION 5 – DRAFTING THE POLICY
        a) A title for the policy? – whole group
        b) Staff work on selected policy headings –
           pairs or individually

4.00   SUMMARY AND ACTION PLAN

Figure 0.1
The Head's hasty plan for
the INSET day on
Speaking and Listening

Session 1 – Introduction

9.00 am
Everyone has a copy of the school prospectus open in front of them. They are looking at the school's statement of values and objectives. They are brainstorming ideas as to how these apply specifically to pupils' Speaking and Listening skills. There is no shortage of ideas. (See Figure 0.2.)

LEARNING FOR LIFE

VALUES

and want to talk about
their world and listen to it   *confidence to speak*

WE BELIEVE that a good school develops (confidence and self-esteem) in its pupils. It produces children who are curious and caring about the world around them, inspired to learn and (courteous) and tolerant in their relationships with each other and with adults.   *in speech and action*

How do we address adults? Which adults? Learning about appropriate speech

A good school is one which sets and maintains high standards for all of its members, both children and staff. It recognises that a child learns (courtesy) and (care) (commitment) and (integrity) (tolerance) and (responsibility) from personal experience of these qualities in adults close to them, both at home and in school. A good school recognises that a child learns to value others by being valued himself/herself, regardless of race, creed or culture.

Does our speaking and listening put some cultural norms   *all of these have*
ahead of others, e.g. standard English?   *a verbal dimension*

Are we missing 'speaking' skills
here, or are they not as basic as
literacy or numeracy

We believe that a good school embraces, and yet aims beyond, sound literacy and numeracy skills for its pupils. The good primary school promotes a sense of belonging in its children and their families. In partnership with parents, it recognises that the cultivation of a positive and enthusiastic attitude to learning, sound (social skills), and personal qualities of (honesty) (kindness) and (self-discipline) provide a sound basis for future success and happiness in the lives of its pupils.

Speaking and listening!

AIMS

At MURRAYVILLE PRIMARY we aim to   *no shouting!*

nurture warm and mutually respectful relationships among adults and children, and a (calm) purposeful atmosphere in which children feel safe and supported

provide a curriculum which is broad, balanced, stimulating and challenging and related to the wider world in which speaking and listening are crucial life skills

recognise individual needs and offer equal opportunities to all

use a well-structured, thematic approach to learning which allows children to appreciate the natural links between subject areas as well as the subjects by themselves

value the *process* of learning, and the skills involved, as well as the *product*

encourage and praise children wherever possible

encourage children to aim high and ("have a go") *In S×L too*

teach children to (reflect) on their own learning in order to value their own achievements, set new targets and make sound choices   *verbally?*

Figure 0.2
Brainstorm on the school prospectus

asking questions

teach children to become independent learners who are able to access the information needed to complete a task, able to explore and investigate, and motivated to do so

provide opportunities for (teamwork) so that children may enjoy co-operating with, and learning from each other — *needs S&L skills*

provide a sense of community in which good citizenship, and respect for people and property, are encouraged

value each child, and every child's contribution, including (out-of-school interests) activities and achievements

drama club, french club...
S&L skills

be there to support children and their families whenever needed

welcome regular communications and involvement with parents and the wider community

practise constant reflection, a systematic review of our curriculum and performance, and a programme of staff development and appraisal.

kids showing visitors round the school

9.45 am

The results of this general open-ended discussion session are:

■ eight empty coffee mugs

■ five minutes of therapeutic moaning about trainers whose heads are full of jargon but fail to help Heads whose days are full of hassle

■ five minutes of less therapeutic moaning about how kids are not prepared to listen any longer

■ a list of questions. (See Figure 0.3.)

- Do we value speaking and listening sufficiently?
- How can we find out?
- Is our approach to speaking and listening too haphazard and informal?
- How can we find out?
- How do we respond to the National Curriculum in this area?
- Do we need a specific policy document?
- Do we need a curriculum co-ordinator?
- What does our contract with the event leader say about non-appearance?

Figure 0.3
Key questions

9.50 am
Everyone agrees that an effective policy document is essential and that to identify its key features should be the main aim of the day.

The Head reminds the staff of her 'policy on policies'. They should not just enshrine the present but point to the future.

Session 2 – The National Curriculum

10.00 am
It doesn't take the Head long to find the only really useful task in the pile of paper sent by the absent event leader. It seems an ideal way into the National Curriculum part of the discussion. It's a simple exercise which involves taking statements from the National Curriculum (as in Figure 0.4) and placing them on a scale from 'strongly agree' to 'strongly disagree'.

Figure 0.4
Positioning these cards on a scale of 'strongly agree' to 'strongly disagree' led to useful discussion

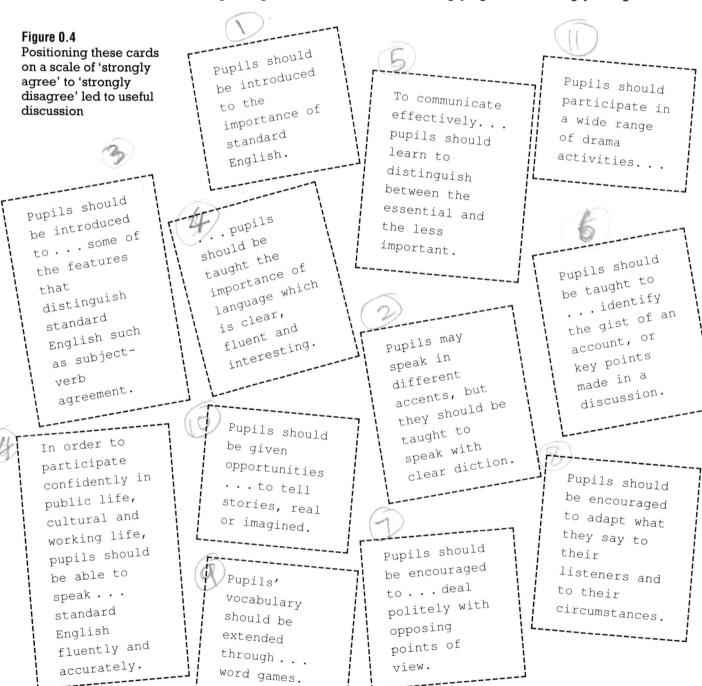

Pupils should be introduced to the importance of standard English.

To communicate effectively. . . pupils should learn to distinguish between the essential and the less important.

Pupils should participate in a wide range of drama activities. . .

Pupils should be introduced to . . . some of the features that distinguish standard English such as subject-verb agreement.

. . . pupils should be taught the importance of language which is clear, fluent and interesting.

Pupils should be taught to . . . identify the gist of an account, or key points made in a discussion.

Pupils may speak in different accents, but they should be taught to speak with clear diction.

In order to participate confidently in public life, cultural and working life, pupils should be able to speak . . . standard English fluently and accurately.

Pupils should be given opportunities . . . to tell stories, real or imagined.

Pupils should be encouraged to adapt what they say to their listeners and to their circumstances.

Pupils' vocabulary should be extended through . . . word games.

Pupils should be encouraged to . . . deal politely with opposing points of view.

Mrs Marsh deals out the cards to each person. Each member of staff then places their cards in turn on the scale as they think appropriate. Once all the cards have been placed, the discussion can begin in earnest as everyone responds to the statements and to the positions they have been awarded. A group consensus will be attempted, with cards moved as appropriate.

10.05 am
Mr Bennett suggests the exercise is a waste of time.

'It doesn't matter at all if I agree with a statement,' he says. 'If it's in the National Curriculum then OFSTED will be looking for it when they inspect me so I have to do it. Waste of time . . .'

The Head reminds him that according to the sage words now emanating from the DFE the new National Curriculum is a framework and it is the teachers' professional role to make it teachable. It is the teachers' role to decide what should receive most attention in their school and what should receive less attention. Moreover OFSTED will be looking to see if they have exercised their professional judgement in this delicate matter.

'OK! You're the boss!' says Mr Bennett and the exercise begins.

There's much descriptive and explanatory language in placing the statements: 'I'll put it here because . . .' Then debate and discussion take off as the group attempts to achieve a consensus, and the typical conventions of adult speaking and listening are in evidence – turn taking, clarifying, rephrasing, questioning others as well as a little verbal bullying and closed ears.

10.35 am
They end with a fair consensus. The greatest difficulty is caused by the term 'standard English' because the staff cannot really agree what it is.

Various alternatives such as 'appropriate English', 'common English', 'shared English' and 'accurate English' are suggested.

It is pointed out that although the National Curriculum states that standard English is distinguished by its vocabulary and by forms and conventions of grammar, it also allows that these may break down in the spontaneity of speech. The Head moves things on by suggesting that as a rule of thumb they are aiming for children to be able to express themselves clearly and concisely using language which will be understood wherever English is spoken.

'It's a bit rough and ready as a definition, but this is a rough and ready sort of day!'

10.45 am
Now it's time for some self-assessment. Everyone should relate the National Curriculum statements to their own teaching, listing those areas where speaking and listening are explicitly valued, and noting where more can be done.

Ten minutes of quiet thought and list-making follow.

Mrs Cooper asks for clarification: 'I presume this applies to the whole curriculum, not just the National Curriculum?'

'Of course.'

11.00 am

The staff are pooling their ideas. They are in reporting mode. There are some concise summaries. There is also much backtracking and rephrasing (some are happier with this kind of speaking than others; just as you would find with a cross section of pupils, in fact). Some teachers use a chart to structure their reporting back (see Figure 0.5). Others improvise from a few brief notes. Others confine themselves to a very straightforward description.

Questionnaire?
Think of a child
in your class.
...... to ......
do they do
regularly?

Figure 0.5
Using a chart to report back to the group: an example

	SPEAKING	LISTENING
ALREADY EXPLICIT (but how focused? How do we assess it? Do we value it?)	– *describing the weather* – *sharing news* – *reading aloud* – *presenting class assembly* – *end of term drama production*	– *story time LOTS!!* – *information* – *class and whole school assembly* – *register*
COULD DO MORE	– *explaining work to others and to visitors* – *describing science experiments* – *debating*	– *make more use of school radio?* – *at story time could listen for more specific things . . . use predicative strategies*

11.35 am

Now it's time to draw the threads together. The clear consensus is that there is a lot of Speaking and Listening activity taking place.

'Surprise, surprise!' says Mr Bennett.

Even so, these activities are not given particular prominence in anyone's planning. Various reasons (excuses says Mrs Andoh) are put forward for this:

■ most children can speak when they get to school

If there *is* any problem, it's a medical one or one needing specialist treatment

■ children pick up what they need as they go along

■ there's no time to concentrate on Speaking and Listening

■ there are other more important areas of the curriculum

■ parents want to see their children's books – you can't show them a discussion.

Taking another tack, Mrs Wise points out that we ask our children to do more listening than speaking and that although the National Curriculum allows for the close interrelationship between speaking and listening, most of the requirements of the orders are about speaking. There is actually very little about listening.

'Obviously modelling ourselves on SCAA and the DFE,' says Mr Bennett.

11.55 am

It's up to the Head to summarise. The more the staff talk, the more they are adamant that Speaking and Listening is a fundamental area of the curriculum, upon which almost all other teaching depends.

'It's like writing,' says Mrs Hughes. 'You can't do without it – but you can't measure it and you don't do it for its own sake.'

There is general agreement that 'doing it for its own sake' is not the aim. And even if the school wanted to, it would be a mug's game finding the extra time.

'It's not an extra scheme of work we need or even more time. We just need to be aware of what we do already and make better use of those opportunities. Be more focused. This is why we need a policy for Speaking and Listening. The policy should be part of the English co-ordinator's brief but, because this skill is so basic to every subject, we all need to contribute to the policy. We each need to draw the implications of it not only into our own class teaching but into the other policies for which we are responsible.'

12.00 midday

The staff can see a faint smile on the Head's lips. Everything seems to be slotting into place quite neatly. The Head suggests tasks for the rest of the day:

■ **Session 3** Until and over lunch Key Stage groups will find illustrations of how the NC aims can be made explicit rather than implicit across the whole curriculum.

■ **Session 4** After lunch they will feedback the group's ideas then each apply this to one half-term planning sheet.

■ **Session 5** For the rest of the day they will identify the key concerns that each element of the S and L policy should address; tackling, in particular, the most problematic area of the policy – equal opportunities – or as the Head puts it 'Access to all the curriculum for everybody'.

Session 3 – Key Stage Groups

12.05 pm

The Key Stage groups have started work. The Head has a second to reflect.

During the morning the conversation had stopped and started, meandered then rushed forward. At times it had broken up into three or four separate streams which then joined together again. It has been calm at times, at others almost violent. They have all employed the skills of speaking and listening, the very complex skills of tone, negotiation, expression and clarity which they hope their children will learn and develop including a few skills (cutting ripostes, sarcastic put-downs, angry silences) which they hope they will not.

The Head's secretary interrupts her thoughts. It's the phone. It's the trainer or the non-trainer.

'Nothing serious.' He sounds husky, but she's had teachers struggle through a day in school who had a quarter the voice. 'Shall I come along for the afternoon?'

'Don't worry Mr Gummer. You get a good rest,' she says with some delight.

They're doing very nicely without him thank you. *Even so*, she muses as she puts the phone down, *the day so far has shown how much we expect of children when we tell them to 'Get into a group and . . . '.*

Lunch

1.30 pm
The Key Stage groups are still writing up their ideas as a series of more organised bullet points to hand on to the English co-ordinator.

Session 4 – Feedback

2.00 pm
Everyone is back together again and agrees that the day has been going well. There's a real sense that what's happening is connecting very firmly with the teachers' everyday needs and experiences.

The Key Stage groups start to share their work.

Their pointers to the future include examples such as:

■ using choral speech as an aid to reading and story

■ focusing on language when conducting and reporting science experiments

■ equipping children better to talk about their feelings

■ encouraging structured debate and discussion

■ using role and drama more in history

■ using story to introduce scientific concepts

■ developing accurate descriptive language in study of places in geography

■ encouraging children to speak poetry and prose in more diverse and exciting ways

■ linking the expressive arts in a more 'home grown' Christmas performance

■ making better use of school radio and audio resources.

2.30 pm
To consolidate these discoveries each staff member applies them to a single, half-term planning sheet (fig 0.6).

2.45 pm
They decide not to feed back verbally but to pass their examples to the Language co-ordinator to help her in her work on the policy.

Figure 0.6
Half-term planning sheet

Class: Term: Teacher:

TOPIC NAME
or HEADING to catch the children's interest
(Explanation in brackets as necessary)

STARTING POINT
What things/activities/role-play/visits, etc.,
are going to be the starting point for the
topic?

PURPOSE
What subject (Sc, Hi, Ge) is central to the
theme? What other curriculum areas
support the theme?

OTHER CURRICULUM AREAS
What subject areas could enhance this
main theme?
Where does Information Technology fit into
the theme?

TIME

FINISHING POINT
What form does the FINISHING POINT take?
(Exhibition; Display; Performance; Assembly;
Check list; Works of Art; Quiz for others;
Book Arts – topic book, newspaper.

THREADS
THREADS/THEMES/PROCESSES
Environmental awareness, PSE, Health Ed.,
Citizenship, Media Ed., Equal Opps
(Gender, Multi-cult.), Aesthetic,
Business

Session 5 – Drafting the Policy

3.00 pm

A lot has been achieved but there's now a sense of weariness. Actually writing the policy is going to be someone else's problem. So what more is there to do today? 'What shall we *call* this policy?' the Head asks. 'Oddly, it doesn't appear so simple after all.'

It's Mrs Andoh who gets everyone buzzing again. She talks about some of the new words her class came up with when they were asked to describe tastes:

'Poppyfizz' for sherbet, 'Clingsweet' for candyfloss, 'Fullbread' for naan bread and so on.

There's some general discussion of children's inherent love of spoken vocabulary; for complicated, even convoluted words and tongue twisters ... (And, comments the Head, their interest in new swear words.) The variety of dinosaur names which children learn and relish is cited. But do we capitalise on this in school? There's fun and creativity inherent in so much speaking and listening, how can the policy reflect this?

'Couldn't we give our policy an expressive, product name – to show it is all new, all speaking, all listening.' The suggestions begin:

'Wordwise,' says Mrs Bales.

'Speakclear,' says Mrs Cooper.

'Hearsay,' says Mrs Wise.

'Speako,' says Mrs Cooper, 'teaches better with new standard English accelerator.'

Mr Bennett suggests a competition for the best name (with a special bonus for silliness) 'Speakeasy', 'Claptrappings', 'Big Ears'. Silly, but it does raise the energy level enough to make the last session work.

3.10 pm
Things begin to move on. It's felt that the policy shouldn't be seen only as 'the written policy', as if an idea's legitimacy is only apparent once it's written down. This process, the discussion and thought, the planning and evolving, is to be seen as an important part of the Speaking and Listening policy. The written document will record, but the living interaction of ideas will sustain the working out and application of the policy in the day to day life of the school. It's important to keep in mind that the staff do not create policy for 'them' (OFSTED, the Head, future readers, the governors); rather the policy relates first to what actually happens or what could happen. It is about the children and their needs. In essence, this policy is for the children.

3.20 pm
In pairs, the staff focus on a couple of the broad policy headings used by the school:

- values and aims
- using this policy document
- the whole curriculum
- organisation and teaching
- management and co-ordination

- assessment, recording and reporting
- resources
- equal opportunities
- special needs.

Large sheets are given out for the staff to work on and the rest of the afternoon is spent in brainstorming, refining and fleshing out ideas. The results are variable but stimulating (see Figure 0.7).

VALUES AND AIMS

Children are natural communicators – we aim to harness that natural skill and enhance their learning.

Aims?
1 Equip for world of work
2 Equip for social interactions – with children and adults
3 Enable to talk about feelings and inner life
4 Assist creativity
5 Learning through talk
6 Small group work – essential in adult life
7 Relationship between speaking and literacy

Talk as a way of reporting results and conveying findings
Do we want a speaking code for school, as we have a uniform code?

USING THIS POLICY DOCUMENT

– need to decide who it's for – teachers, pupils or parents? As this will affect style. Title: could be catchy one which pupils could also relate to. SPEAKEASY is not such a bad idea!

To express its dynamic; could use a word bubble approach

Two characters (boy + girl) to sum it up
[Clear Mouth + Big Ears]

each point in policy to be a question being put by a parent, with answers from the children

Could be written so it sounds as if it's being spoken – do it as a dialogue?

Figure 0.7
The results of brainstorming on the
school's broad policy headings

17

THE WHOLE CURRICULUM

The National Curriculum gives directions to the S+L policy – but it is not all of it.

NB French club, drama club etc also figure

All parts of curriculum (and all policies) need to be informed by S+L policy

Recognise that conversing with parents, watching TV is influential.

ORGANISATION AND TEACHING

Probably not a useful heading for this particular policy but could say

– for all curriculum need to organise the learning experience so that pupils' speaking and listening skills are encouraged.

– also something about paying particular attention to getting pupils to speak in group work.

Need to say too:

– like writing, S+L are basic skills . . .

MANAGEMENT AND CO-ORDINATION

English co-ordinator has prime responsibility for monitoring implementation, subject co-ordinators need to

– build in S+L concerns at planning stage

– develop progressive and developmental action plan which links across subjects so that vocabulary development is co-ordinated

ASSESSMENT, RECORDING AND REPORTING

Do we add a heading as S+L in the school report – a general heading not under English?

Need a flexible, standard assessment sheet to help monitor a pupil's contribution to small group and large group discussions

What do we show the parents?

maybe not we but they, the children

Parents' evenings could include a verbal report prepared by the pupil with exhibits from his/her work that term. Let the medium be the message.

RESOURCES

Physical
tape recorders
speaking books
video recorders/television
radio
computer
telephone

need to look again at what
school's TV and radio do

why do computer voice synthesisers always
sound so flat, but CDRom can sound great ?

Human
visitors

NB we could write our resources
under other curriculum headings e.g.

Maths – tables;
History – oral history, etc

Books

poetry

story

drama ideas

Media

Pupils to be encouraged to keep a week's diary of their media
use – what radio do they listen to, etc? audio diary would fit
purpose better.

EQUAL OPPORTUNITIES

Recognise how in adult mixed-sex conversation a woman who speaks as much as a
man is judged to be 'taking over'.
Gender is a real issue in S+L.

Note where there are genuine language difficulties because of culture – English as a
second language.

SPECIAL NEEDS

Sign language?
What research done into overcoming extreme shyness?

Summary and Action Plan

4.00 pm

The Head sums up the action plan:

1 Each subject co-ordinator will consider the implications for their own policy.
2 Staff meeting time will be set aside in four weeks to enable staff to update colleagues on their progress.
3 Mrs Andoh, as English co-ordinator, will draft the School's S and L policy, including sections on assessment, equal ops, differentiation, resources in the light of today's discussion and her own knowledge of practice/resources in the school from her monitoring role. This will be discussed and ratified in six weeks' time.

4.15 pm

Now everyone goes off to plan tomorrow's work, put up display boards, update today's records and . . .

5.50 pm

It's only as the Head is packing up at the end of the day that she notices again a question on one of the first brainstorms of the morning:

'What does our contract with the event leader say about non-appearance?'

Indeed! What does it say? She begins to search out the contract, but almost as soon as she opens the filing cabinet, her memory clicks into focus . . . . She's at a Heads' forum and Julie Phillips, fellow Head, is saying to her, 'Make sure you get a signed contract from old Gummer. He never sends them out. And make sure when you phone him that you tie him down to specifics, he's an absolute devil. With his writing royalties he's not so bothered any longer . . . and when he does turn up he's so damned brilliant that he gets away with it.'

So there was no written contract and, as the Goldwynism goes, 'a verbal contract isn't worth the paper it's written on'. Sorting out the repayment of the fee would be complicated to say the least. When she'd phoned Gummer she had been in the middle of the usual school rush and hadn't planned properly what she wanted to say. If only she'd listened to Julie.

How to use the material in this book

1. As a curriculum planning tool

The bulk of this book is made up of practical activities. They are divided into seventeen units. We have gathered the units into those particularly suitable for Y1/Y2 (units 1–6), those most suitable for Y3/Y4 (units 7–11), and those most suitable for Y5/Y6 (units 12–17). This structure will illustrate some of our assumptions about progression in Speaking and Listening skills – for example our assumption that small group discussion can become increasingly effective and independent at the upper end of the age range. It will be immediately obvious, however, that these age-bands are very loose. Every unit, and indeed almost every activity within every unit, could be adapted for use in a younger or older age group.

The seventeen units show how you could have a Speaking and Listening focus once per term throughout Key Stages 1 and 2. It is vitally important, however, to stress that they do not form a scheme of work for Speaking and Listening. Rather they form an attempt to illustrate how Speaking and Listening skills can be identified and encouraged within your existing curriculum provision and (where necessary) injected into it if you feel that there is more you can do in this area.

The overall requirements for Speaking and Listening in the National Curriculum are summarised in the following diagram.

Summary of revised orders

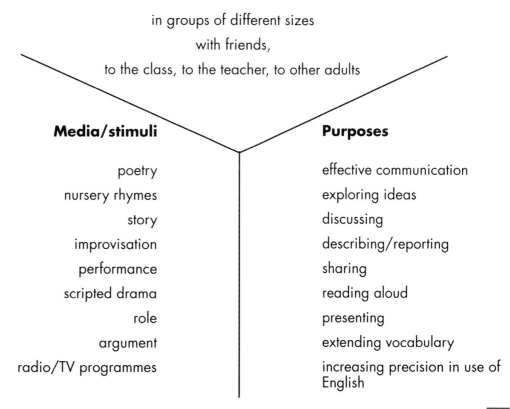

Contexts

in groups of different sizes

with friends,

to the class, to the teacher, to other adults

Media/stimuli	**Purposes**
poetry	effective communication
nursery rhymes	exploring ideas
story	discussing
improvisation	describing/reporting
performance	sharing
scripted drama	reading aloud
role	presenting
argument	extending vocabulary
radio/TV programmes	increasing precision in use of English

In our planning of the seventeen units we have attempted to ensure that through the Key Stages 1 and 2, children's Speaking and Listening skills should be developed:

■ in a range of pupil contexts (in pairs, in small groups, in large groups etc)

■ using a range of stimuli or media (drama, poetry, story etc)

■ for a range of purposes (formal, informal, instructive, exploratory etc).

As you analyse your own school's provision for Speaking and Listening you can use a similar diagram to help ensure that you are providing a broad range of opportunities for children to develop their Speaking and Listening skills.

2. As a bank of ideas

The units can be used as they stand or adapted.

Each unit has a similar structure; see the sample unit on page 24.

Most units are broken down into a number of distinct activities which can be extracted to stand alone, and can be easily adapted for other needs and situations. To this end all the activities are separately listed and indexed – along with other important topics – on the page opposite.

Index

Curriculum context
This indicates the curriculum area to which these activities most apply. However – as with most Speaking and Listening activities – there are almost always significant applications to other areas. These are explained at the end of each set of activities in 'Developing this work . . . .'.

Key Strategies
Each of the units focuses on a particular Key Strategy – e.g. using Story or using Drama. This section highlights the key features of the strategy and it's potential for developing pupils' speaking and listening skills, and relates them to the 'range' statements in the National Curriculum.

Expected outcomes
Whilst one cannot predict the outcomes of most Speaking and Listening activities, this feature identifies which of the 'key skills' from the National Curriculum are most likely to be developed by these activities.

How to use the material
We have presented these activities as ready to use. However, we are aware that most teachers will adapt the materials very freely – and use the parts that fit their teaching and learning schemes. This section therefore highlights particular considerations that you will need to bear in mind in adapting or using the material.

You will need
Lists equipment or resources you will need to prepare in advance.

A Sample Unit

UNIT 1

Dragons

MAKING A PERFORMANCE POEM

Curriculum context

Mainly English within this unit, although there are possibilities for developing poems such as this on a range of themes. Page 43 lists opportunities for using these structures in Science, Geography and History based topics.

Key Strategies

Poetry was a spoken medium before it was a written one, and the current vogue for performance poetry is a welcome rediscovery of this. Everyone will, however, have experienced flat or stilted poetry reading. To overcome this children do need encouragement to speak poetry boldly and with conviction. It can be helpful, particularly with the infant age group, to abandon the printed page and use the pupils' own poetry – especially if that poem is custom-designed for speaking out loud.

In this set of activities pupils will:

■ build up a simple class poem

■ add sound effects to the poem to create a 'sound picture'

■ 'perform' the poem.

Expected outcomes

■ increased ability to speak clearly and confidently

■ a sense of shared creativity and celebration

■ enhanced vocabulary

■ experience of a variety of poetic forms and structures

■ imaginative uses of language.

How to use the material

The material is presented as a series of activities building one on the other. As with all the ideas in this book, however, the individual activities can be used in any way that seems appropriate. They can also easily be adapted for small groups, or individual work.

The activities could be used over two sessions, with a break after Activity 3, but they could also be split into more and shorter sessions.

As always, the length of the sessions will be determined by your own approach, the concentration span of your class, and their responses to the material.

NB: Some writing ability is needed for Activity 3, but suggestions are given for how this can be accomplished with groups of varying ability.

You will need

■ equipment to make the poem board (Activity 3).

39

The Strategies

Activity title	Key Strategy	Curriculum context	Tips for . . .	Resources
Section 1 – Y1/Y2				
1. Dragons	**Poetry and sound pictures:** making a class poem for performance	English	. . . making a poem board	Dragon poem Dragon description
2. A Bun for Barney	**Story**: listening skills **and Drama**: choral speaking and making sound effects	English Maths	. . . focused listening	A Bun for Barney as a) a story and b) a play
3. Sink or Float	**Structured talk:** conducting and reporting an experiment	Science	. . . assessing pupils' S and L skills	Report sheets (2) Assessment sheets (3)
4. Long Ago	**Composite**	History		
5. The Rockets	**Story:** listening to and responding to a story	English	. . . handling difficult feelings . . . story telling	Space Race story Ice-Cream delivery story Feelings dance
6. Underground	**Movement**	English Science		Script for underground movement
Section 2 – Y3/Y4				
7. Christmas	**Drama:** still pictures into living pictures	English RE	. . . making still pictures	
8. Jealousy	**Composite**	English PSE		Jealous feelings monologue Jealousy poem
9. Hanuman	**Puppets**	English RE	. . . developing puppet dialogue	The story of Hanuman Outlines for stick puppets
10. Parents and Grandparents	**Interview**: gathering oral history evidence	History	. . . oral interviews	
11. The Forest People	**Drama**: teacher in role	English Geography	. . . teacher in role	
Section 3 – Y5/Y6				
12. Saying 'No'	**Drama**: Forum Theatre	English PSE	. . . using Forum Theatre	
13. Fear	**Composite**	English PSE		Fear poem
14. Ecology	**Debate**: structuring a class debate	English Geography	. . . running a class debate	
15. Evacuees	**Drama**: small and large group play-making	History	. . . role work . . . Conscience Alley	
16. Design a Playground	**Interview**: conducting a research interview **Presentation**: presenting research findings	Design and Technology		Sample questionnaire Sample running order
17. On Air – Radio News	**Presentation**: a radio feature	English Media Education	. . . news bulletins	Planning sheet Running order Sample script Tips for news teams

3. To identify Speaking and Listening opportunities within your own curriculum

Every unit has a particular curriculum context which is identified at the start. Each unit also concludes with suggestions as to how the strategies used could be developed in a range of contexts.

However, these suggestions are only the beginning. One of the most useful activities which this book could stimulate would be a brainstorm by all staff for how Speaking and Listening skills could be further developed in a range of curriculum contexts.

For example, our own brainstorm produced the following list. Where the idea is further developed in the units a cross reference is included.

Cross-curricular links

Science

Use listening to sounds as an integral part of scientific investigation and observation. (See p. 61.)

When recalling places that have been visited, use the creation of sound pictures as an aid to recall. (See p. 43.)

Investigate how sounds are reflected and absorbed in different environments. (See p. 62.)

Encourage active listening when children are describing scientific processes or experiments. For example, when children are describing how to look after a pet, ask the rest of the class to keep a mental note of facts relating to food, water and shelter.

Encourage children to listen to the sounds of their environment. (See p. 62.)

Children can investigate the sounds made by different objects and develop a vocabulary to describe the differing qualities of the sounds.

Listen to the different tonal qualities of voices in the class or on tapes of people whom the class do not know. (See p. 62.)

Children could make a radio or TV advertisement (either recorded or dramatised) about how we should look after the countryside.

Looking at how a seed turns into a plant, children could observe a growing plant weekly and talk about its shape, size, colour and smell. Encourage descriptive language, record it and compare each week's words at the end of the term. (See p. 61.)

Build a drama around a class trip to the moon. The events of the drama can be exciting and imaginative, whilst the structure of the journey could be built around the scientific reality of such a mission. Ensure that such words as Earth, Moon, orbit, gravity and zero gravity are understood.

Encourage structured reporting back of scientific experiments. (See p. 61.)

Maths

Tell stories which have a counting element in them so that children can join in. (See p. 49.)

Children can work in pairs, back to back. One child draws a shape and then explains to his or her partner how to draw it. The partner attempts to draw while listening. Encourage detailed descriptions and careful listening.

Children can create scale maps of imaginary treasure islands. They then give a photocopy of their map to a partner and guide the partner to the treasure. The complexity of the instructions will vary with age and ability but could include scale distances ('30 metres north from the big rock') and the use of degrees to determine angles.

Listen carefully to sounds then put them into sets:

inside sounds	outside sounds	
		sounds made by living creatures
		sounds made by non-living things

Build poems with a clear mathematical structure – the first verse having one line, the second verse having two lines and so on. (See p. 44.)

Use times tables as the structure for a poem. (See p. 44.)

Tell stories in groups about the journey of an insect and set in the actual classroom. The story could be accompanied by a detailed plan with measurements. (See p. 55.)

Encourage verbal reporting back of mathematical investigations.

History

Create sound pictures to represent particular historical episodes. (See p. 43.)

Encourage children to listen to music from the period that you are studying. (See p. 73.)

Invite a guest whom the children can listen to and question, someone who remembers the Second World War or the moon landings, for example.

Record two different accounts of the same event on tape. Question the children about what they have heard and explore how there can be different interpretations of the same event.

Tell historical stories. A vast amount of investigation, comment and role work can flow from an engaging story.

When children write first person accounts of, for example, a Roman childhood, a Saxon invasion, or living through the Blitz, they can read these out to the class and answer questions in role. (See p. 165.)

Documents can be useful starting points for exploring historical incidents through drama.

Develop class poems with rhythms influenced by the historical setting: for example, a factory rhythm with added machine sounds.

Use Forum Theatre (see p. 139) as a method of exploring moments of decisions in history. For example, should the Iceni fight the Romans or try to make peace?

Geography

Children can work in pairs; one child acts as the guide, the other is blindfolded and has to follow the guide's instructions through an obstacle course or maze. If several pairs work at once, the blindfolded ones will need to home in on the appropriate 'guide voice'.

When children draw maps of places that they have visited they could note on their maps the sounds which can be heard there.

Make tape recordings of contrasting areas of the school. Can children identify areas from their sounds alone?

When recording or describing weather, use comments about the sounds made by the weather. (See p. 43.)

When studying the weather children can tell stories in which the weather plays a part.

Weather poems can be particularly effective, especially if they are spoken chorally with added sound effects. (See p. 43.)

Invite different people who work in the school (for example, the caretaker, dinner staff, the cook, cleaner, teacher, helper, or secretary) to say a brief word to the class about what they do. Encourage focused listening by giving the children things to listen for.

Working in pairs, one child describes a scene which the other can't see. The listener attempts to draw it from the description. The description needs to be as detailed as possible and is an excellent way to introduce geographical terms related to buildings, roads, hills, rivers, etc.

There are variations on this:

■ the listeners can be allowed to ask questions

■ the task could be based on a familiar scene, such as a part of the school which the describers know well or have drawn in advance. Can the listeners identify which part of the school is being described?

Small groups of children could answer questions from the rest of the class about the school. The rest of the class imagine that they have never seen the school and the group in the 'hot seat' gives as much information as possible about the location, locality, size and buildings, etc.

After a visit run a class discussion about the place or building just visited. Focus and structure the discussion by asking the children to think up categories for the discussion, for example, the journey, first sight of Haddon Hall, the surroundings, the history of the buildings, the most interesting bit of the day, the least interesting bit.

Use drama to create a community which lives in a certain type of geographical location. (See p. 130.)

Speaking and Listening games

Below is a selection of games which use and develop speaking and listening skills. The games are not targeted at any particular Key Stage, but are offered for teachers to use and adapt as appropriate.

Listening games

Guess the sound

Place: Classroom, fairly close together.
Equipment: A number of things that make a sound.

Children all close their eyes while you make sounds with various objects which they then have to guess. An alternative is for you to make the sounds under a covered table, but this may muffle the more delicate sounds.

Everyday objects which you can use include:
   Sticky tape pulled from reel
   Vibrating ruler
   Scissors
   Stapler
   Pencils rattled
   Chalk on board
   Knives and forks
   Paper torn
   Book leafed
   Ball bounced

Sound effect story

Place: Small groups in classroom.
Equipment: Various objects for sound effects.

Working in pairs or small groups, children secretly choose a story well known to the class. They then choose sound effects from the story and work out how to make them.

When each group is ready, they perform their sound effects and the rest of the class try to guess the story that they come from. It might be best to listen to the sound effects with eyes closed to increase the illusion.
Possible stories are:
   Red Riding Hood
      Footsteps in wood
      Growls
      Ticking clock (bedroom)
      Axe
      Groans (wolf)

   Carrie's war
      Medley of air raid and war effects

   The Lion, the Witch and the Wardrobe
      Roar
      Cackle
      Squeaky door

Keeper of the keys

Place: Children sitting in a fairly large circle on the floor.
Equipment: Noisy bunch of keys, optional chair.

One child is the keeper of the keys. She sits, with eyes closed, in the middle of the circle, either on a chair with a bunch of keys beneath, or on the floor with the keys in front.

A child from the circle is silently chosen to attempt to steal the keys and return to their place with them.

The keeper can try three times to point to where she thinks the thief is, in an attempt to catch her before the keys are successfully stolen.

Grandmother's footsteps

Place: Large cleared space, could be outside.
Equipment: None.

In this well known playground game, 'Grandmother' stands at one end of the space with her back to everyone else, who all start from the other end. The children must attempt to creep up on Grandmother who periodically turns around, particularly if she hears movement. If she sees anyone move they are sent back to the start.

The child who gets close enough to touch Grandmother on the back becomes the new Grandmother.

Captain's coming

Place: Large cleared space.
Equipment: None.

The children spead out in the space.

You call out various commands, each of which has an appropriate action. For example,

Trim the sales – mime climbing rigging

Scrub the deck – mime scrubbing deck

Lifeboats – mime rowing

Port – All run to left

Starboard – All run to right

Submarine – Lie down with one foot in the air (periscope!)

Captain's coming – stand to attention and salute.

As the game progresses, increase the frequency of the commands to try to catch the children out.

Traffic Lights

Place: Large cleared space.
Equipment: None.

A simpler version of Captain's coming, this game develops the same skills in younger children.

You call out GREEN – Move (or later a specific movement such as jumping or skipping)

RED – Stop

ORANGE – Which can indicate a chosen action which you decide in advance, or 'free movement'.

Salad

Place: Children on chairs in a circle.
Equipment: None.

This is a lively game which calls for very focused listening. Give everyone the name of part of a salad, repeating the same four or five ingredients as you go round the circle: Lettuce, Cucumber, Tomato, Onion, Lettuce . . .

Everyone has a chair except for one child who stands in the middle. The child in the middle calls out one of the salad ingredients at which point all the other children must get up and find a new chair. The one in the middle is also looking for a chair and if he or she finds one, then there is a new person in the middle to call the ingredient for the next round.

To develop this, allow children to call more than one ingredient at a time, and to call 'Salad' as a cue for everyone to change places.

Battleship and Submarine

Place: Children standing in a circle.
Equipment: None.

Choose two children to stand in the middle of the circle. One is the Battleship, the other the Submarine. Each chooses a controller. The two vessels close their eyes or are blindfolded. They move only where their controllers tell them to with instructions such as Forwards, Backwards, Left, Right, Stop.

The Battleship must keep away from the Submarine whose task is to collide with the Battleship to end the game. Everyone around the edge is a mine and if either vessel touches a mine it explodes.

The Battleship can win by luring the Submarine onto a mine or by surviving for a preset time.

For those unhappy with the military imagery, play Sheepdog and Sheep with the rest of the class as an electric fence!

Concentration games and ice breakers

Grand old Duke

Place: Children standing in a circle with space between.
Equipment: None.

Children will need to be very familiar with the rhyme, The Grand Old Duke of York.

They sing it several times to establish a common tempo and rhythm. It can help if they swing one arm as they sing in order to keep the rhythm for what is to come.

Next try singing it without the word 'up', so everyone just leaves an appropriate pause at that point.

Next try without the word 'down'.

Then try without either 'up' or 'down'.

My Bonny

Place: Children standing in a circle with space between.
Equipment: None.

Children need to learn the song, My Bonny Lies Over the Ocean. They sing it several times for familiarity and establishing tempo. Everyone puts their hands out in front, arms stretched, hands making a fist with thumbs up.

They sing the song, and every time they sing a word beginning with the letter B, they reverse their thumbs. So

My Bonny lies over the ocean (thumbs down on 'Bonny')

My Bonny lies over the sea (up again on 'Bonny') . . . and so on.

In the lines with lots of Bs the concentration needed to follow the Bs and not the rhythm of the song is considerable.

After trying it with thumbs, attempt the same thing with two body positions, crouched down, and standing with arms outstretched. Apart from anything else, it's very good exercise!

I love you honey . . .

Place: Sitting in a circle.
Equipment: None.

One child turns to the left and says to the child next to her, 'I love you honey but I just can't smile.'

This is then passed on right around the circle.

The game is to try to say it with a straight face!

You have to choose your group carefully for this as some will make no attempt to keep a straight face, in which case the game becomes an excuse for silliness!

Name exchange

Place: Enough cleared space for everyone to stand and move around.
Equipment: None.

Everyone stands in the space and on your cue they move around, shaking hands with everyone they meet.

As they shake hands they say, 'Hello, I'm . . . who are you?'.

They then take on the name of the person they have just met and move on to the next person.

The concentration comes in trying to remember who you are when you keep changing names.

Imaginary ball

Place: Children sitting in a circle on the floor.
Equipment: None.

Throw an imaginary ball around the circle. This is a good way for new class members to learn everyone's name, as you say the name of the person before throwing the ball to them.

You can complicate it by having two different sorts of imaginary ball (say a tennis ball and a football) in action at once.

Word games

Story pairs

Place: Children sitting in pairs, at tables or on the floor.
Equipment: None.

In pairs children tell a story taking only one word each. It can be either re-telling a well known story, or making up a story from scratch.

Story circle

Place: Children sitting in a circle either as a whole class or in small groups
Equipment: Optional 'speaking gourd'

Children take it in turns to tell part of a story before passing on to the next person.

You can use a 'speaking gourd', which is any object which permits only the holder to speak. If using this, anyone can put up their hand to receive the gourd and thus continue the story.

Find out about . . .

Place: Children working in pairs.
Equipment: None.

Children work in pairs to find out as much as they can about their partner before presenting this information to the rest of the class.

Pass a message

Place: Children spread out in pairs in a large cleared space.
Equipment: None.

Children sit with a partner, all except a small number (up to four, but experiment for the best result), who are guards.

When you start the game the partners each try to pass a secret message to each other while the guards patrol the space. If the guards see anyone talking, they can order the offenders to the side of the space.

Uses for . . .

Place: Children in discussion area.
Equipment: An empty tin, bottle, sock, or other object.

The situation is that you are all marooned on a desert island, in a deep forest or on an uninhabited planet.

The only object you have is a tin, a bottle or whatever. The class have to think up as many practical uses for the object as possible. Encourage them to think laterally; just how many uses can they find?

Descriptions

Place: In pairs in a large cleared space.
Equipment: Objects, maps, paper and pens.

Children sit back to back. One child draws a shape, then describes it to the other child, who draws as they listen. This encourages careful descriptive language. The same technique can be used for describing an object (the partner draws what is described) or taking a journey over a map both partners have. Older pupils could even describe a geographical scene from a photograph while the other attempts to draw it.

Join the club

Place:	Children sitting in a circle.
Equipment:	Optional pencil, crayons etc.

One child leaves the room and the rest choose one simple requirement that is needed to 'join the club'. It could be sitting with your arms folded, or holding a pencil upside down, or scratching your nose when you talk etc.

The child comes in and asks, 'Can I join the club?'

Everyone else is sitting appropriately, or with the correct object and the questioner must keep asking to join the club, trying different positions etc, until he or she gets it right.

You can make it more complicated by having false clues such as everyone holding coloured pencils which actually have nothing to do with the requirement.

Another version involves having only some of the class doing the correct thing so that the questioner asks, 'Can Rachel join the club? Can Satnam join the club?' etc, and works out the requirement from the answers.

Imagined journeys

Place:	Large, cleared space.
Equipment:	Gym equipment optional.

Working in pairs, one partner closes their eyes and is guided by the sighted partner who leads them on an imaginary journey around the space.

'You're about to enter a deep cave, careful it's slippery . . . ' etc.

As they lead their partner, they can use gym equipment as part of the experience.

'Feel this smooth tree trunk, you'll have to stoop down to get under it . . . '

My name is . . .

Place:	Children sitting in a circle on the floor.
Equipment:	None.

Each child introduces himself/herself. The first says her name. The second, her name and the previous name.

'My name is Rowena and this is Charlotte.'

The third adds her name and recalls the other two, and so on.

Grandmother went to market

Place:	Children sitting in a circle.
Equipment:	None.

The first child says,

'My Grandmother went to market and she bought . . . ', adding her own idea. The second child adds her own idea and repeats the first, and so on round the circle.

A variation is to require each new word to begin with the letter or sound which ended the last word so the sequence might go: coat → turnip → personal hi-fi . . .

STRATEGIES AND ACTIVITIES FOR Y1/Y2

Dragons

MAKING A PERFORMANCE POEM

Curriculum context

Mainly English within this unit, although there are possibilities for developing poems such as this on a range of themes. Page 43 lists opportunities for using these structures in Science, Geography and History based topics.

Key Strategies

Poetry was a spoken medium before it was a written one, and the current vogue for performance poetry is a welcome rediscovery of this. Everyone will, however, have experienced flat or stilted poetry reading. To overcome this children do need encouragement to speak poetry boldly and with conviction. It can be helpful, particularly with the infant age group, to abandon the printed page and use the pupils' own poetry – especially if that poem is custom-designed for speaking out loud.

In this set of activities pupils will:

■ build up a simple class poem

■ add sound effects to the poem to create a 'sound picture'

■ 'perform' the poem.

Expected outcomes

■ increased ability to speak clearly and confidently

■ a sense of shared creativity and celebration

■ enhanced vocabulary

■ experience of a variety of poetic forms and structures

■ imaginative uses of language.

How to use the material

The material is presented as a series of activities building one on the other. As with all the ideas in this book, however, the individual activities can be used in any way that seems appropriate. They can also easily be adapted for small groups, or individual work.

The activities could be used over two sessions, with a break after Activity 3, but they could also be split into more and shorter sessions.

As always, the length of the sessions will be determined by your own approach, the concentration span of your class, and their responses to the material.

NB: Some writing ability is needed for Activity 3, but suggestions are given for how this can be accomplished with groups of varying ability.

You will need

■ equipment to make the poem board (Activity 3).

ACTIVITY 1 Dragon talk

WHERE?   In the story corner, or sitting in a circle.

HOW?   To introduce the theme of the poem, begin with discussion about dragons.

- What do children know about dragons?

- Do they know any stories which feature dragons?

- What do dragons look like?

- Can they be friendly?

- Where do they live?

Try to draw out the common threads, e.g.:

- dragons fly

- they breathe fire

- they live in caves

- sometimes they guard treasure.

Also use this discussion to encourage the children to build up dragon pictures in their minds. Encourage descriptions of:

- the colour of dragons

- their shape

- the sounds a dragon might make as it flies across the night sky or guards its treasure.

Encourage children to describe the mood and atmosphere surrounding a dragon. You could read a 'Dragon' poem or story if it helps pupils to catch the mood and atmosphere. An example is given on the resource sheet.

At this stage the aim is not to create a single picture of a particular dragon in a specific situation, but to focus the children on the subject.

ACTIVITY 2 Dragon words

WHERE?   Around working tables or desks.

HOW?   Split the class into groups. Each group's task is to come up with its own list of 'dragon words', growing out of the 'Dragon talk' activity. Encourage the groups to write down as many words as possible but to produce only one list of words per group.

This activity involves some writing ability so each group will need a 'scribe' who can write confidently. Alternatively:

- With a group where all the children can attempt writing, the list could be passed from child to child. The aim is get some discussion going, though, so avoid a situation where each child takes a turn and then sits back until their go comes around again.

■ In a group with less-able writers, the task might be to think up or remember as many words as possible until the teacher or another adult comes to write the words down for the group. A cassette recorder might be helpful here for those who find writing laborious. They could record their ideas orally whilst still excited about the task and transcribe them later at a slower pace – with or without support.

■ In a class where the task would be too demanding for groups, an alternative approach is to sit the whole class in a circle around a large sheet of paper on which you have already drawn the outline of a dragon. Then, as children suggest words or phrases, you write them down, asking the class the best position in each case.

Activity 3 Dragon 'sound picture' WHOLE CLASS DISCUSSION

WHERE? In the story corner, or sitting in a circle.

HOW? Begin to focus the discussion on one particular scene – which can be imagined by the whole class together – perhaps a dragon flying, or sleeping in its cave, as in the example below. The aim is to build up a 'sound picture' of the scene.

Read aloud the following description on the resource sheet, asking the children to recall the sounds mentioned.

Once the children have remembered a good number of sounds, and added some of their own, go through them one by one, asking the class to vocalise the sounds with you.

You may wish to bring in percussion instruments at this stage. You could try a low wind in the caves (vocal), water dripping (vocal or percussion), treasure chinking (percussion or everyday objects) or snores (vocal).

Add some shape to the sounds if this is appropriate, helping, for example, to give the breathing sounds peaks and troughs, or encouraging a less regular pattern of chinking for the treasure sounds.

NB: You will probably need a time-gap between Activities 3 and 4 in order to prepare the poem board, or you will need to have prepared it in advance.

ACTIVITY 4 Class poem

WHERE? In the story corner, sitting where everyone can see the 'poem board'.

HOW? Use a 'poem board'. This is a simple piece of equipment that can be used again and again in this type of activity.

◆ *Tips for. . .* **making a poem board**

- Use a flip chart or a large sheet of strong cardboard or wood covered in paper so that it can be used again and again.

- Prepare a number of slips of thin card each with one of the children's 'dragon' words from Activity 2 on one side and blu-tack or similar on the reverse.

- Also on card prepare some clear, simple symbols representing the different sounds created in Activity 3; e.g. a drop of water, wind, treasure, Dragon, breathing smoke.

Now the class work together on their poem. Go through the words and ask the children to suggest a good word to start with. Stick it to the board with blu-tack, leaving enough room at the left hand edge for one of the sound symbols to be added later.

It might be that your next word is also from those that have been prepared, but you also have the option of writing directly on the board, adding verbs to make sentences if appropriate. In this way you gradually build up a poem.

You can increase the complexity of the poem as appropriate to your class. You could also decide to start with a given structure for your poem. For example, it will have two verses of four lines each, with each verse ending with the same short phrase. Whatever parameters you set, it's important to remember that this poem will be performed by the whole class.

Once you have the words, the class can think about which sounds will accompany them and you can place the appropriate symbols alongside each line.

ACTIVITY 5 Performing the poem WHOLE CLASS PERFORMANCE

WHERE? In the story corner or somewhere where everyone can see the poem board.

HOW? Decide who will say each line. For variety, it is good to have some parts spoken by individuals and others by the whole class.

To avoid the poem board becoming too crowded, you could simply draw around the words or phrases that the whole class say, asking individuals to remember which parts they read. The process needn't exclude non-readers since some individual parts could be an easily learnt phrase or word.

Now, the big moment for the class, when they first try out their poem. Be ready to conduct, encourage and rehearse the class. The children will get a real sense of achievement as their performances improve.

Stand the group up for one last run-through at full volume.

An excellent way to finish the project would be to share the poem with the rest of the school in an assembly.

Development across Key Stages 1 and 2...

SUBJECTS FOR OTHER CLASS POEMS AND SOUND PICTURES There are many subjects from other curriculum areas which particularly lend themselves to the creation of class poems and sound pictures. For example:

■ **Weather** For Science or Geography, pupils can create a class poem which describes a particularly windy day, a cold frosty day, a snowy day, a steaming hot day, etc. Encourage children to consider the sound a particular type of weather makes; sometimes rain goes 'pitter patter', sometimes it's more like sitting under a shower on full blast.

■ **A Place** In Geography children are expected to develop a sense of place. A class poem, based on a sound picture of a place, is an ideal vehicle to develop and describe places, including imaginary ones. See how far the children's imagination can take them in building up a sound picture of a place such as a Brazilian shanty town, a high Himalayan village, an Arctic settlement or a New York street.

■ **Our visit to . . .**   Similarly, after a class visit to a museum, a theatre, a park, etc, pupils can use 'sound pictures' to create a class poem which conveys their experience on the visit. This is an original way to report back to the rest of the school.

■ **History**   Create sound pictures or class poems to represent a place or event that pupils are studying. For example, Saxon villagers building a settlement; Vikings at sea in a long boat; a factory in the Industrial Revolution. The rhythm of the poem or sound picture could be influenced by the historical setting. The 'Saxon villagers' sound picture could be based on different building rhythms such as hammering, sawing, and digging. The 'Vikings' sound picture could be based on the slow powerful rhythm of rowing and the 'Factory' poem on the incessant, rapid clacking of the spinning or weaving machines.

OTHER STRUCTURES FOR POEMS

Not all class poems need to be built around 'sound pictures'. You could build them around a clear mathematical structure – for example:

■ **Cumulative poem**   The first verse must have one line, the second verse two lines and so on. You could base these poems on memory games such as 'My grandmother went to market and bought . . . ' (See p. 35.)

■ **Times table poem**   Use times tables as the structure for a poem. If you sit in a circle and allow each child to choose the object of each verse, you can create an instant poem along these lines:

> One elephant times two is two elephants,
> Two giraffes times two is four giraffes
> Three geese times two is six geese . . .

You can then develop this so that each line is followed by a 'tag line':

> One elephant times two is two elephants,
>   and they're big!
> Two giraffes times two is four giraffes,
>   and they make holes in the ceiling!
> Three geese times two is six geese,
>   and what a noise they make!

Develop poems around the idea of symmetry, perhaps using 'In the Mirror World', as the title. These poems could be written in a symmetrical shape, and/or performed with two voices, giving a symmetrical pattern to the performance.

OTHER USES OF POETRY

■ **Nursery rhymes**   Games which use nursery rhymes to develop pupils' Speaking and Listening skills can be found on pages 32 and 33.

■ **Raps**   Older children can use the strong rhythmic structure of the rap as the basis for a class poem – particularly one which tells a story. It is not so useful for setting a mood because the strong rhythm tends to overshadow the language.

SEE ALSO

■ **Units 2, 8 and 14**   for other uses of poetry to develop Speaking and Listening skills.

Resource 1

Dinosaur skin
Bat-like wing
Fish-like fin.

Fire breather
Treasure seeker
Flying creature.

Seen at night
Sky's alight
Then gone from sight.

Dragon flashes by
Dragon flying high
In my mind's eye.

The dragon is sleeping in his cave deep underground. There are many passages above him, winding their way through the hard, dark rock. The dragon feels safe in his warm cave, dozing on his pile of gold and jewels, heated by the hot rocks below. It's a tight squeeze for such a large creature to twist his way through the winding narrow passages that lead from the surface. No human has ever come this far, but if they did, they would see nothing, for no light comes through from the world above. They would see nothing, but they would hear . . . what would they hear?

The drip, drip, drip, of distant water as it falls from a crack in the roof?

The chink, chink, chink, of treasure as the Dragon shifts his mighty weight, moving in his sleep?

The deep, long snores of the sleeping creature?

The gentle hiss of steam escaping from his nostrils?

The distant sound of wind echoing in the passages above?

A Bun for Barney

STORY

Curriculum context

This is essentially an English-based activity. The story on which it is based, however, includes simple counting and the suggested activities take in Dance, Drama and PSHE.

This is one of a number of activities in this book which use stories as the basis for pupil work.

Key Strategies

This example emphasises developing children's listening skills, allowing them to listen with a purpose (to predict the turn a story might take) and then to use choral speaking and sound effects to retell the story.

Expected outcomes

■ enjoyment of the story!

■ shared sense of involvement and creativity in taking part in a performance

■ enhanced listening skills

■ opportunities for creative talk

■ clearer diction through choral speaking.

How to use the material

The activities in this unit are based around the excellent story for young children, *A Bun for Barney*. The full text of the story is reproduced here with thanks to the author and publisher.

If the book is not already in your school library, we recommend it. The layout and illustrations make it ideal for reading to a whole class as well as with early readers. The illustrations are very well suited for discussion in small groups or one to one situations. The details of the book are: Joyce Dunbar, *A Bun for Barney*, Orchard Books, ISBN 1-85213-037-7.

In Activities 1–3 we offer a number of simple ideas for using the story to help children to listen carefully, and to identify the engaging word patterns.

Activity 4 develops the story into a class performance including mime, choral speaking and sound effects.

You will need

■ percussion

■ copies of drama version.

Resource 2

(page breaks in the original are indicated by a line)

A Bun For Barney

by Joyce Dunbar

Barney the bear had a bun.

It was an iced currant bun with five cherries on.
Barney said, "An iced currant bun with five cherries on will go down nicely in my tum."
And he settled down to eat his bun.

But before he could take a bite a wasp came whizzing and buzzing.

"Will you please go away," said Barney, "and leave me to eat my bun."

But the wasp buzzed louder and said,
"Yes, if you give me a cherry."

So Barney gave the wasp a cherry.

"Oh well," he said with a sigh, "an iced currant bun with four cherries on is better than a bun with none."

He was about to take a bite when a mouse came mooching and munching.

"Will you please go away," said Barney, "I'm trying to eat my bun."

But the mouse muttered and said,
"Yes, if you give me a cherry."

So Barney gave the mouse a cherry.

"Oh well," he said with a sigh, "an iced currant bun with three cherries on is better than a bun with none."

He was about to take a bite when a crow came croaking and cawing.

"Will you please go away," said Barney, "I want to eat my bun."

But the crow cackled and said,
"Yes, if you give me a cherry."

So Barney gave the crow a cherry.

"Oh well," he said with a sigh, "an iced currant bun with two cherries on is better than a bun with none."

He was about to take a bite when a squirrel came scrabbling and scratching.

"Will you please go away," said Barney, "I'm longing to eat my bun."

But the squirrel squeaked and said,
"Yes, if you give me a cherry."

So Barney gave the squirrel a cherry.

"Oh well," he said with a sigh, "an iced currant bun with one cherry on is better than a bun with none."

He was about to take a bite when a fox came sniffing and snouting.

"Will you please go away," said Barney, "I'm bursting to eat my bun."

But the fox snarled and said,
"Yes, if you give me the cherry."

So Barney gave the cherry to the fox.
"Oh well," he said with a sigh, "an iced currant bun is better than none."

Then Buster the bear came along.

"GO AWAY!" said Barney.

Buster the bear growled and said,
"Yes, if you give me the bun."

"No," said Barney to Buster, "for this iced currant bun with no cherries on is going
   going
      going
         going . . .

GONE!"

And it went down nicely in his tum.

ACTIVITY **1** During the story

WHERE? In the story corner or the assembly area as appropriate.

HOW? The high quality of this story makes it easy to encourage careful listening. Children across the infant age range are instantly engaged by it. They quickly catch on to the story's rhythm and structure, instinctively joining in with the recurring elements. Because the animals and the number of cherries change each time, however, the children have to 'keep with' the story, rather than relying on automatic repetition.

To enhance the counting element of the story you could:

■ make a card bun with detachable cherries

■ as the cherries disappear, ask the children to hold up fingers for the correct number of cherries.

◆ *Tips for. . .* **focused listening**

None of us find it easy to listen for long. Children in particular need help – more than just being told to sit still and listen!

■ Before you start the story give the children something to listen for. It can be anything: 'What noise does the squirrel make when it approaches Barney?' If each child in the class has something different to listen for it will increase the value they attach to the activity. At the end of the story, or at an agreed point en route, ask for their ideas.

■ If there are repetitive devices in the story encourage children to join in and say these lines together. For example, in *A Bun for Barney* 'An iced currant bun with – cherries on is better than a bun with none.'

■ Warn children in advance that you are going to make one deliberate mistake. At the end of the story you are going to ask them what they think it was so they will have to listen carefully.

■ Stop your story at regular intervals and ask the pupils to join in with appropriate sounds, for example, in *A Bun for Barney:*

Stop each time a new animal is introduced and encourage the children to join in with the appropriate sound:

wasp – whizzing and buzzing

mouse – mooching and munching

crow – croaking and cawing

squirrel – scrabbling and scratching

fox – sniffing and snouting

Buster – growls

ACTIVITY 2 Thinking about the story DISCUSSION ABOUT ISSUES

WHERE?   In the story corner.

HOW?   You can use the story to discuss coercion, bullying, friendliness and generosity. Use questions such as:

- Should Barney have given all his cherries away?

- Were the animals right to ask for them?

- Did they 'ask nicely'?

- Why did Barney say 'GO AWAY' to Buster?

- Was it hard for Barney not to give Buster the bun?

- How did he find the courage to refuse Buster?

- What would have been the fairest thing to have done with the bun?

If you are using the illustrated picture book, you can ask the pupils the following questions:

- Who else shares the first part of Barney's journey until she flies off with a cherry?

- Can you see each new animal in the picture before he or she speaks to Barney?

ACTIVITY 3 Extending the story STORY-TELLING SKILLS

WHERE?   Individually or in small groups at their tables.

HOW?   This story can stimulate pupils to write their own Barney stories:

- They could extend this story. What other creatures might come to ask for a cherry or a piece of the bun? What noises would they make and how would they move?

- They could say what happened before the story. How did Barney get the bun in the first place?

- They could tell the next episode in the story. How might Barney behave the next time that he goes walking with something to eat?

- They could fill in detail in the story. What different places does he go to as he tries to eat his bun? Where does the journey start and end? If they tell their ideas first, they can then compare their ideas with the illustrator's if you have the illustrated version.

ACTIVITY 4 Acting out the story

WHERE? In the school hall or a cleared space in the classroom.

HOW? This simple dramatisation gives most of the class a choral role in repeating the phrase, 'Yes if you give me a cherry'. The children also provide the sound effects for the different animals, count down the number of cherries, and verbalise Barney's final stand when he eats the bun.

There are individual roles for seven children as Barney and the six animals he meets.

It could easily be expanded. You could:

■ Split the choral sections so that different children take different parts. This would allow you to expand the choral sections without individual children having too much to remember.

■ Add percussion and other musical elements to the various animal sounds. This would also allow the animal movements to be extended and perhaps developed into a simple dance.

■ Add more children to each animal section so that, for example, a number of crows enter and nudge one of their number forward to ask for a cherry. They might exit arguing over the cherry.

■ If you have strong readers, you could split the actual narration between them, or give more of the story-telling over to choral speaking.

Resource 3

A Bun For Barney

by Joyce Dunbar

Characters (*in order of appearance*)
Barney the bear
A wasp
A mouse
A crow
A squirrel
A fox
Buster the bear

TEACHER:	Barney the bear had a bun. *Child enters as Barney, skipping along carrying his bun*
TEACHER:	It was an iced currant bun with . . . *Children join in the counting*
TEACHER:	One, two, three, four, five cherries on. Barney said, An iced currant bun with five cherries on will go down nicely in my tum. *Barney mimes rubbing tum*
TEACHER:	And he settled down to eat his bun. *Barney sits down to eat his bun. He rubs his tum again and is about to take a huge bite when . . .*
TEACHER:	But before he could take a bite a wasp came whizzing and buzzing. *A child enters as a wasp buzzing around the space. The children make wasp sounds*
TEACHER:	"Will you please go away," said Barney, "and leave me to eat my bun." *Barney shoos the wasp away*
TEACHER:	But the wasp buzzed louder and said,
CHILDREN:	Yes, if you give me a cherry.
TEACHER:	So Barney gave the wasp a cherry. *Barney gives the wasp a cherry and the wasp buzzes off. The children make buzzing sounds*
TEACHER:	"Oh well," he said with a sigh, an iced currant bun with *Children join in the counting*
TEACHER:	One, two, three, four cherries on is better than a bun with none." *Barney counts the cherries and is about to take a bite when . . .*

TEACHER:	He was about to take a bite when a mouse came mooching and munching. *A child enters as a mouse, scurrying about the space. The children make squeaking noises*
TEACHER:	"Will you please go away," said Barney, "I'm trying to eat my bun." But the mouse muttered and said,
CHILDREN:	Yes, if you give me a cherry.
TEACHER:	So Barney gave the mouse a cherry. *Barney gives the mouse a cherry and it exits with more squeaking from children*
TEACHER:	"Oh well," he said with a sigh, "an iced currant bun with *Children join in the counting*
TEACHER:	One, two, three, cherries on is better than a bun with none." *Barney counts the cherries and is about to take a bite when . . .*
TEACHER:	He was about to take a bite when a crow came croaking and cawing. *A child enters as a crow, pecking and strutting around the space. The other children make crow noises*
TEACHER:	"Will you please go away," said Barney, "I want to eat my bun." But the crow cackled and said,
CHILDREN:	Yes, if you give me a cherry.
TEACHER:	So Barney gave the crow a cherry. *Barney gives the crow a cherry. Crow exits, more crow noises from children*
TEACHER:	"Oh well," he said with a sigh, "an iced currant bun with *Children join in the counting*
TEACHER:	One, two, cherries on is better than a bun with none." *Barney counts the cherries and is about to take a bite when . . .*
TEACHER:	He was about to take a bite when a squirrel came scrabbling and scratching. *A child enters as a squirrel, scrabbling and scratching around the space. The other children make squirrel noises*
TEACHER:	"Will you please go away," said Barney, "I'm longing to eat my bun." But the squirrel squeaked and said,
CHILDREN:	Yes, if you give me a cherry.
TEACHER:	So Barney gave the squirrel a cherry. *Squirrel exits. More squirrel noises*

TEACHER: "Oh well," he said with a sigh, "an iced currant bun with
Children join in the "one"

TEACHER: One cherry on is better than a bun with none."
*Barney counts the cherries and is about to take a
bite when . . .*

TEACHER: He was about to take a bite when a fox came
sniffing and snouting.
A child enters as the fox sniffing around the space

TEACHER: "Will you please go away," said Barney, "I'm *bursting* to
eat my bun."
But the fox snarled and said,

CHILDREN: Yes, if you give me the cherry.

TEACHER: So Barney gave the cherry to the fox.
*Barney hands over the cherry and the fox exits
looking pleased with itself*

TEACHER: "Oh well," he said with a sigh, "an iced currant bun . . .

CHILDREN: . . . is better than none."
Barney is about to take a bite when . . .

TEACHER: Then Buster the bear came along.
*A child enters as Buster who stomps about the
space looking menacing. The other children make growling
noises*
"GO AWAY!"
said Barney.
Buster the bear growled and said,

CHILDREN: Yes, if you give me the bun.
*Barney hesitates, then slowly stands up and faces
Buster. During the following he moves the bun
ever closer to his mouth and on each "going"
takes a bite, until on the "gone" he finishes the
bun and rubs his tum.*

TEACHER: "No," said Barney to Buster, "for this iced currant bun with
no cherries on is

CHILDREN: *joining in and getting louder with each word*
going
going
going
GONE!"

TEACHER: And it went down nicely in his tum.
*Barney walks off rubbing his tum!
Buster remains, looking across.*

Development across Key Stages 1 and 2...

USING STORY TO COMMUNICATE CONCEPTS

There are many curriculum areas in which concepts can be communicated well by a simple repetitive animal-based story structure such as *A Bun for Barney*.

A single character might be set up to run through the stories. For example in Science a dog might be used to explore:

■ **Changing materials**   A dog goes searching for its rubber bone – finds it first squashed underneath its owner's foot, then stretched in a struggle with another dog, then bent around the branches of a tree, but it always returns to the same shape. Then he tries the same with his stick and discovers that it is not so malleable. Children then retell the story with other materials to explain how they would change.

■ **Grouping materials**   The dog is trying to get comfortable – he tries lying on all sorts of materials and gradually sorts them into various piles according to texture, how soft they feel, etc. Children retell the story to use different systems of classification.

■ **Forces and motion**   The dog, increasingly mischievous, has decided to drag all the things he wants into his den. He starts with simple objects which can be carried, then moves on to balls which must be pushed or rolled, and bigger objects such as pillows, etc which must be pulled. Children continue the story to include as many different forces as possible for the dog to use.

IN MATHS

■ **Measurement**   Develop a class story about the journey of an insect around your classroom. The story is to be accompanied by a detailed plan with measurements.

When the story is read out or told, the story-tellers move about the space demonstrating where the various incidents happened. For example, 'The ant walked 30 centimetres up the side of the gerbil cage . . . '

SEE ALSO

■ **Units 5 and 7,** which also focus on using story.

Sink or Float

STRUCTURED TALK

Curriculum context

This is a Science-based activity which focuses on children working in small groups; first in an unstructured way, then in an increasingly structured context.

Although this particular experiment examines 'sinking and floating', the aim is to provide a set of strategies which can guide children's Speaking and Listening in any Science experiment. Assessment sheets are included to help you monitor children's speaking and listening skills as observed in a range of contexts.

Key Strategies

In popular imagination the stereotypical scientist works on his or her own, in a laboratory, making wild inventions. Most scientific work in fact is collaborative – and requires the full range of Speaking and Listening skills.

In this activity children will:

■ work in small groups on a Science experiment

■ take part in informal discussion

■ predict, observe, and describe what they see

■ present their ideas to others using simple and clear descriptions and explanations.

Expected outcomes

■ enhanced scientific vocabulary

■ confidence in small group/whole class discussion

■ understanding of the need to organise and structure their reporting back

■ increased precision in choice of words

■ opportunities for assessment of pupils' Speaking and Listening skills by the teacher.

How to use the material

The four activities are all based around experiments in which the children play with water.

Unlike with some of the activities in this book it would be difficult to miss out any stages as they build on each other. The activities do, however, need to be spread over a period of time as they require small groups each to have time in the water play area.

These are deliberately simple activities based around work which many teachers will already be undertaking in the course of their regular teaching.

At each stage of the activities we have explored the assessment opportunities they present. At the end of the unit a sample Assessment

Chart is offered which may be photocopied or adapted to your requirements – allowing you, or a colleague observing with you, to record what you see and hear.

You will need

- water toys
- report sheets.

ACTIVITY 1 Water play

SMALL GROUP PLAY/DISCUSSION

WHERE? In a water play area.

HOW? Small groups of children play with various water toys.

This activity should be organised so that over a period of time, say a week, every child has the opportunity simply to play with the toys. These could include boats of various kinds, paddles, water wheels, etc. It is also important to have some objects which do not float, perhaps even have boat shapes which sink! Have some 'toy people' in the water as well as objects to encourage imaginative play.

There are obvious practical considerations of classroom management to consider and you may need a parent, or other helper, to assist. The play will provide a 'raft' of common experience and fun which can be used effectively in the activities which follow.

The objective is for children to engage in casual talk as they discuss what they are doing together. They may make up stories involving the toys; they may dispute over who plays with what; they may negotiate with others and so on.

ASSESSMENT OPPORTUNITIES Choose three or four children whose Speaking and Listening you intend to assess during these activities. You could use Assessment Sheet 2.

■ Look at how each child has listened to your explanation of the task, and put your instructions into practice.

■ Listen to their 'casual interaction' as they play with the water toys. Are they playing using imaginative speech? 'Look out, we're sinking . . . '

■ Can they negotiate for what they want?

■ Do they listen to one another?

ACTIVITY 2 Water talk

WHOLE CLASS DISCUSSION

WHERE? In your usual discussion place but out of sight of the water toys.

HOW? Have a general discussion with the class about the water play.

The idea is to encourage children to:

■ describe the toys they have played with (keep them out of sight so that children cannot simply point to them)

■ talk about how the water behaved in the toys (as in a water wheel) and how the toys behaved in the water

■ begin to talk about the properties of the water they played with: cold, wet, drippy, splashy, etc.

This should be a gentle discussion in which the children recall their enjoyment of the water as well as reveal their understanding of its properties.

Now move the discussion on by talking about things which floated in the water and those which did not. Reveal the water toys one by one and try to get a class consensus about each toy's ability to float. Designate one table a 'Floating things' area, and another a 'Sinking things' area and ask the children to place each object on one of the tables after the class have discussed its properties.

NB: You may also need a 'Sometimes float' table, for those toys which float at first then sink as they become waterlogged. If this seems to confuse things too much, try to eliminate such toys before the children play with them!

ASSESSMENT OPPORTUNITIES To assess individuals in this kind of class discussion, it is best to observe whilst the talk is led by a colleague, and to focus on just a few children. You could use Assessment Sheet 2.

■ Focus on the range of descriptive words employed by each child. How appropriate are their descriptions? Do they offer a clear picture of the object/event being discussed?

■ Try to keep a simple tally of the frequency of contribution or attempted contribution (acknowledging that a child may often put up their hand but not be selected to contribute verbally).

■ Assess the vocal clarity, in technical terms, of each child you are studying. Are they loud enough when they speak in this way? Do they speak clearly?

■ How distinctly do the individual children express their opinion as to which category the objects should be placed in?

Activity 3 Sink or float

WHERE? In an area with water.

HOW? You can now formalise the earlier work by setting up an experiment in which small groups test whether each of a given set of objects sinks or floats.

Again you will need to stagger the times, but as there are a set number of simple tasks (we recommend four objects to test) groups will need less time at the water tray than in Activity 1.

Give each group two report sheets, one with 'Sink' and the other with 'Float' at the top. Photocopiable sheets can be found on pages 63 and 64. As pupils conduct the experiment, they can write or draw the object on the appropriate sheet. Keeping these sheets dry will provide a genuine experimental difficulty – you could laminate them and use an acetate-type pen, or you could attach the sheets to clipboards fixed down well away from the water.

ASSESSMENT OPPORTUNITIES These are as for Activity 1. You could use Assessment Sheet 1.

ACTIVITY 4 Sink or float?

WHERE? It depends on whether you favour a general discussion or more formal reporting. To observe and develop presentational speaking and listening skills properly it might be advisable to set up a more formal reporting procedure – each group must say clearly how they tested the objects and what the results were.

HOW? Reporting back can be quite demanding for young children. Prompt their report with questions to provide a structure:

■ What did you have to find out?

■ How did you find out?

■ Where did you do your experiment?

■ Can you show us which things floated?

■ Can you show us which things sank?

This approach can help to encourage a sense of scientific procedure.

If speaking to the whole class adds too much to the tension and difficulty, each group or individual can come one at a time to speak to the teacher.

ASSESSMENT OPPORTUNITIES If you use one-to-one reporting, or groups reporting to the whole class, you will be able to do the assessment as the child reports; perhaps use Assessment Sheet 3 as the child talks to you and then write a brief comment afterwards.

Focus on the structure of the child's responses:

■ To what extent are they able to answer your questions succinctly and precisely?

■ Does the child add appropriate and relevant detail to the descriptions and explanations?

If you use whole class discussion for reporting back then you could use Assessment Sheet 1 here as well.

Development across Key Stages 1 and 2 . . .

SCIENCE EXPERIMENTS

A range of Science experiments can be given a similar 'play-discuss-experiment' structure – with opportunities for observation and assessment at each stage.

■ **Materials** Provide a range of materials for children to model with: obvious ones such as plasticene or playdoh, and less obvious ones such as bread dough or potters' clay. Initial play with the materials can be observed, followed by the setting up of a more formal experiment – e.g. which of these models will keep its shape the longest under a heavy weight?

■ **Seeds** Initial play-oriented discussion can focus on a range of seeds: larger ones such as sunflower seeds, conkers, acorns, avocado stones, winged seeds; smaller ones such as grass seeds, apple pips, dandelion seeds, etc. Children can play sorting games, or try making funny faces out of the seeds. The more formal experiment which follows can focus on 'transportation' – how can each of these seeds be moved?

This could be developed by planting some of the seeds and observing how the seed turns into a plant. Children could each have a different seed and report verbally each week on its shape, size, colour and smell. Encourage children to use descriptive language carefully, to record the words they use and, at the end of term, to compare each week's words.

OTHER STRATEGIES FOR REPORTING BACK

With older children in Key Stage 2 you can increase the complexity not only of the experiment but the nature of the reporting back.

For example, you could do this by putting the children into small groups and making each child responsible for one of the following sections of their report:

■ what we were trying to find out

■ what we used

■ how we set up the experiment

■ how we made it a fair test

■ what we expected to happen

■ what happened

■ what we have learnt from this.

OTHER SCIENCE CONTEXTS FOR DEVELOPING SPEAKING AND LISTENING SKILLS

Listening is essential not only to collaborative experiments but to the very nature of scientific observation. So while children use their ears to observe the world around them they can be honing their ability to listen in a focused and concentrated way. For example:

■ Investigate how well toys travel on a smooth or rough surface. Listen to the sounds that the wheels make on the different surfaces. Help children to develop a common vocabulary for describing the sounds – an important aspect of using language in Science.

  Older children might be able to ask if there is any connection between the amount of noise (say from a bumpy cord carpet compared with a smooth floor) that the wheels make and the distance travelled or ease of pushing.

■ On a visit to a park or farm, ask children to take note of the sounds they hear as well as what they see. These could be recorded on a portable recorder or simply noted down, perhaps on a map or plan of the location. The data could be used to create graphs or charts of the natural and artificial sounds heard.

■ Encourage children to listen to the sounds of their immediate school/class environment.

In a quiet place where there is enough space, ask the class to lie on their backs, each child in their own space. They listen first to the sounds outside the room, then inside the room, then to sounds from their own bodies, such as breathing and, if it's quiet enough, the blood in their ears. The simplest way of doing this is to then stop and discuss the sounds which the children have heard.

Another variation is to ask the children to point to where you are as you move about the room, your voice getting quieter and quieter until they only have your footsteps as a guide. This is a good way of settling the class into a listening mode so that they can then focus on the other sounds around them.

■ Ask children to investigate how sounds are reflected and absorbed by talking or making loud sounds (such as clapping) in different environments such as the school hall, the classroom, outside, into a curtain, even under water in a sink (clapping recommended, talking discouraged!).

■ Listen to the different tonal quality of voices in the class, as part of an investigation of diversity and inheritance. Listening with eyes closed is a good idea. Children who have been together for some time will automatically recognise their peers from their voices alone. Can individual children disguise their voices so that the rest of the class don't know who's speaking?

■ To help them identify the scientific laws governing our own planet, as part of a discussion exercise children could imagine the physical laws governing life on a strange planet. Perhaps creatures are born old and grow into babies, plants grow only underground where there is no light, the seas turn solid for one hour at midday . . . and so on. Using talk to create a fantasy world in this way can help to anchor the scientific principles which apply in our environment. You need at least an inkling of what's 'normal' in order to create the unusual or bizarre.

Resource 4

Report sheet 1

Sink

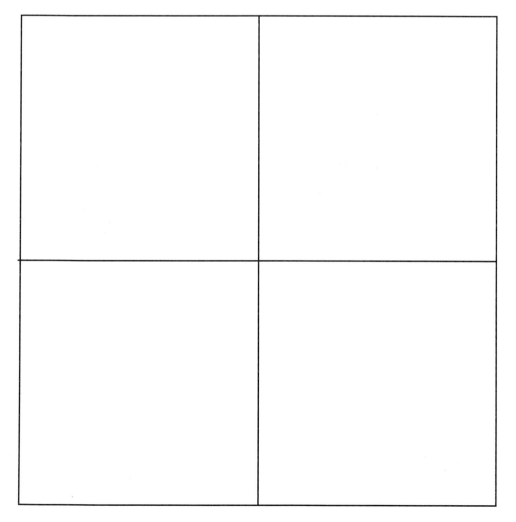

Resource 5

Report sheet 2

Float

Resource 6

Assessment Sheet 1: whole group

NAME:

CLASS: AGE:

DATE ASSESSED:

TASK:

Circle a number (5 = high) as a quick reference, then add a comment in the space below it.

In large groups/whole class discussion

Listens to instructions	1 2 3 4 5
Frequency of contributions	1 2 3 4 5
Vocal clarity	1 2 3 4 5
Succinctness	1 2 3 4 5
Imaginative speech	1 2 3 4 5
Listening to peers	1 2 3 4 5
Confidence	1 2 3 4 5

Comments

Resource 7

Assessment Sheet 2: small group

NAME:

CLASS: AGE:

DATE ASSESSED:

TASK:

Circle a number (5 = high) for quick reference, then add a comment below each entry.

In small groups

Imaginative speech	1	2	3	4	5
Negotiation	1	2	3	4	5
Listening to peers	1	2	3	4	5
Frequency of contributions	1	2	3	4	5

Comments

Resource 8

Assessment Sheet 3: one to one

NAME:

CLASS: AGE:

DATE ASSESSED:

TASK:

Circle a number (5 = high) as quick reference, then add a comment in the space below it.

In one to one situations

Clarity of report	1 2 3 4 5
Organisation of report	1 2 3 4 5
Appropriateness of detail	1 2 3 4 5
Confidence	1 2 3 4 5

Comments

Long Ago

Curriculum context

This is a collection of drama, dance and movement strategies which can be used to start children thinking and talking about significant historical events and using the vocabulary of chronology. The activities will help to set children's study of the past in a chronological framework and enable them to sequence events and objects using common words and phrases related to the passing of time.

Key Strategies

The emphasis is on stimulating children's confidence to participate in large and small group discussion by providing external devices such as dance activities and still pictures (see pages 71–72) to structure their contributions.

Expected outcomes

■ enhanced historical vocabulary

■ imaginative use of language

■ increased confidence in talking in groups of different sizes.

How to use this material

The activities in this unit offer a good starting point for work on any historical project. By making the key phrases (Activity 3) specific to a given History study unit you can place the unit in an overall historical context.

■ The structured talk is based around lively and engaging stimuli.

■ The activities should be done in the order suggested but need not follow one another immediately.

■ The class move from a whole class discussion into a focused, small group task, and then into a structured, solo talk situation.

■ Activity 4 provides the option for a further whole group discussion, built on the previous elements.

You will need

■ timer (for Activity 2)

■ a marker to divide floor space into two (for Activity 4).
In your usual discussion or story space.

ACTIVITY 1 Yesterday, today, tomorrow

WHERE?   In your usual discussion or story space.

HOW?   In a whole class discussion, begin by asking the question, 'Who can tell me about something that they did yesterday?'

Take time to hear a number of replies before moving on to ask, 'Who can tell me about something which they will do (did) today?' Again listen to ideas before moving on to things which children will do tomorrow.

From this discussion ask the children to choose one simple thing each which they can say when you call out 'yesterday', 'today', or 'tomorrow'.

Then call out the words 'yesterday, today, tomorrow' in the correct order a few times. Each time you say one of the words the children should respond all together with their simple phrase.

After saying the words a few times in the correct order, jumble them up so that pupils have to listen carefully for what word you say and choose the correct word from their own three. This should provide a lot of fun as children try to give the correct response. It will be noisy, but the noise will be structured and purposeful!

End this activity by confessing that you have managed to jumble up the order and ask what the correct order of the words should be. Write the words, in order, on the board or have them prominently displayed. Use the written words to reinforce the concept if necessary and then begin to talk about the idea of things which happened lots of yesterdays ago, introducing the concept of 'Long ago' for the next section.

ACTIVITY 2 Long ago

WHERE? In groups around tables.

HOW? In working groups ask the children to identify things which happened, or which lived long ago.

To give structure and purpose to the children's talk you can give them the external 'motor' of a time limit (say one minute) and target; for example, each group should come up with only three things that lived or happened long ago. You can add to the fun of this by setting a kitchen timer or, if you have one, a count-down clock on the computer.

Allow the children to talk and discuss it amongst themselves.

You could, if appropriate, give everyone the first idea – dinosaurs, or World Wars, or children going to work in this country.

When their time is up, ask each of the children to draw one of their ideas ensuring that in each group all three ideas are represented. This will give you an opportunity to help out any group which has found it difficult to unearth three ideas. It also allows you time to assess individual children's contribution to the dicussion and understanding of the concept.

To decide whether a suggestion is admissible:

■ Fantasy elements such as fairy stories which all *seem* to have happened long ago, are perfectly acceptable for the purposes of this exercise.

■ Allow 'borderline' concepts such as 'horses and carts' which still exist and have occasional uses in this country and wider uses elsewhere. The child who comes up with such an idea has focused correctly on something which has vastly diminished in use since 'long ago'.

■ Negatives such as, 'Long ago they didn't have television', would also be good evidence of understanding the concept.

Make time for the groups to talk to the rest of the class about their 'long ago pictures'. Display them so that they can be seen during the next activity.

ACTIVITY 3 Still pictures A

WHERE? In cleared classroom space or hall.

HOW? In this activity, the children work in a space on their own, responding to key phrases from the teacher. All the phrases should be to do with time. For example: 'bed time', 'morning', 'school time', 'play time', 'lunch time', 'home time', 'tea time', 'night time'.

Each child individually forms an instant 'still picture' in response to the key phrase. It should express someone or something that fits the key phrase.

When the 'pictures' are formed, the teacher chooses individuals to say who they are in the picture and what they are doing. The important Speaking and Listening consideration here is for the child to give clear information in the form in which it has been requested. You may feel it is appropriate to stress the two parts of the information you require:

■ Who are you?

■ What are you doing?

This should not be allowed to dissipate the fun of the activity, but be gently urged as appropriate.

Refer back to the earlier discussion and the children's 'long ago pictures' – before moving on to key phrases such as 'yesterday', 'today', 'tomorrow', 'long ago'.

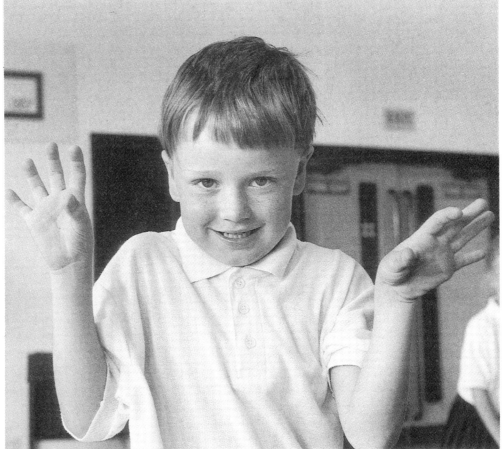

ACTIVITY 4 Still pictures B

WHERE? In the same space, and continuing on from Activity 3.

HOW? This activity flows on naturally from Activity 3 and can be a good way to gain a snapshot impression of what your children know about History and what they have retained from previous work in historical contexts. It can be used to assess their historical understanding and can also lead on to valuable class discussion.

Split the space into two. You could simply use a dividing line on the floor or divide up the space with a PE rope.

Explain that the children are going to make some more 'still pictures' but this time they must decide if the pictures should go in the space called 'today', or the space called 'long ago'. Show the pupils which half of the working area represents each word. You could mark the areas with large signs.

You then proceed as before, but this time give key phrases which relate to work that the children have done previously or that will reveal their knowledge and understanding of History.

You might use phrases such as 'dinosaurs', 'cave people', 'people using computers' (phrased in this way because simply saying 'computers' might be hard for children to realise in a still picture), 'steam engines', 'astronauts' . . . and so on. Pupils will need to listen carefully to your verbal stimulus and move into the correct space to make their still pictures.

As in the previous activity, look closely at a few of the 'still pictures' and ask the children who they are and what they are doing.

Finally it might also be appropriate to broaden this into a discussion – placing some of the 'still pictures' in sequence within the physical representation of time which you have mapped out on the floor.

Discuss:

■ Which came first: dinosaurs or steam engines?

■ Did cave people use steam engines?

■ How could we find this out?

Then ask a few children to recreate their still pictures of dinosaurs, cave people, computers, steam engines and astronauts. Ask the rest of the class to move them into the correct chronological sequence.

Development across Key Stages 1 and 2 . . .

USING STRUCTURED TALK

In the games section there are many suggestions for how pupils' talk can be directed and structured by game devices.

DEVELOPING SPEAKING AND LISTENING IN HISTORY

■ Unit 10, Parents and Grandparents, deals with an oral history project.

■ School Radio drama programmes (see page 183) often include engaging reconstructions of historical events as do, at the time of writing, *Infant History* and *History 9–11*.

■ Encourage children to listen to music from the period you are studying or reconstructions played on similar instruments. Use this listening experience as a building block for drama, prose, poetry or discussion.

■ Encourage verbal reporting back to the whole class of historical investigations. Drama can be powerful here as children use 'still pictures' and 'speaking thoughts' (see page 105), for example, to explain events and dilemmas from history.

Other instances of developing Speaking and Listening in History and the potential for using story and drama in particular, are on pages 121 and 158.

OTHER USES OF THESE STRATEGIES

There is more on using 'still pictures' on page 106.

The Rockets

USING STORY

Curriculum context

These story-based activities are primarily designed for PSHE follow up. However, ideas embracing Science, Design and Technology, Music, Dance and Drama are suggested.

Key Strategies

As pupils listen to stories they develop their ability to listen in a focused way and to respond appropriately. Their ability to recall relevant detail increases and they have the opportunity to compare their reactions to the story with the reactions of other pupils. By entering the imaginative world of a story they can also be encouraged to learn to talk about their own more difficult feelings.

Expected outcomes

■ enhanced vocabulary

■ more focused listening

■ greater ease when speaking about feelings.

How to use the material

This section contains two stories about 'The Rockets' which use a similar format and characters – but for contrasting purposes.

Story 1, *The Ice-cream Delivery*, consciously develops pupils' 'focused listening' skills. Story 2, *Space Race*, uses story to help children to talk about their feelings.

Each story is divided into sections for classroom use and suggested activities relate to these sections. The stories may, however, be copied or used in any other way you wish.

For both stories a range of follow-up strategies are suggested.

You will need

■ pictures of the rockets

■ a 'Mars' and an 'Earth' symbol.

ACTIVITY 1 The Ice-cream Delivery

WHERE? In your story corner.

The story, *The Ice-cream Delivery*, has four characters and two locations. This may make it too complex for very young children, but their ability to focus on the story can be assisted by representing the locations and the characters in a physical way.

THE LOCATIONS The story is divided into sections, depending on whether the action takes place on the Earth or on (or near) Mars. Each section is marked with an 'Earth' or 'Mars' in the top right hand corner.

It will aid children's recall if you have different areas of the story-telling space which you indicate or move to at the appropriate part of the story.

You could have a picture of a blue planet for Earth and a red one for Mars. Or, if you are standing up to read, you could move towards pictures on the wall representing Earth (nature, cities, etc) and Mars (a red planet with two moons).

THE CHARACTERS The story features anthropomorphised rockets. They can be given very clear characteristics and shapes, particularly if you make pictures to represent them. This again will support children's recall.

The rockets are:

■ Yuri the Silver Rocket – a simple, smooth, glistening rocket shape – perhaps decorated with silver foil

■ Helen the Blue Cargo Rocket – a bulkier, heavier craft

■ Buzz the Space Bus – has lots of windows

■ Valentina the Rescue Ship – is very sleek and high tech.

YURI   HELEN   BUZZ   VALENTINA

Tell the story in your usual way, settling the children to listen, pausing to discuss where you feel this would be appropriate and so on.

After the story use the following sorts of questions to assess how closely the children have been listening and what they can recall.

■ Who were the four rockets in the story?

■ What sort of rocket was Buzz? . . . Valentina? . . . Yuri? . . . Helen?

■ Why was Buzz unhappy?

■ Where did Helen go?

■ What was the special cargo that the Martian people were waiting for?

■ What came out of Helen's cargo doors when they were opened?

■ Why couldn't Buzz take off?

■ Who put the rocket fuel in Helen and the ice-cream in Buzz?

■ What happened at the end of the story – how did the Martian people get their ice-cream?

The idea of such questions is simply to assess the children's understanding and recall of the events of the story. This could be done in a whole class group, but you will be able to focus more closely on individual children if you can arrange to speak in small groups.

You can then ask more open questions to encourage the children to respond more imaginatively and at greater length:

■ How do you think Buzz felt?

■ Have you ever had a tummy ache?

■ What words would you use to describe it?

■ How did the Martian people feel when their ice-cream didn't arrive?

■ Have you ever felt disappointed or upset about something like that?

■ Why did Yuri do somersaults at the end of the story?

■ How do you think he felt?

Resource 9

The ice-cream delivery

Earth

5 4 3 2 1 Blast off.

Whoosh! With a sound like thunder Yuri the Silver Rocket blasted off the launch pad and zoomed into outer space at the start of another mission.

5 4 3 2 1 Blast off.

With a gigantic roar Helen the Big Blue Rocket gently lifted off the launch pad and sped off into outer space with her load of ice-cream for Mars.

5 4 3 2 1 Crash, cringle, pop. Wub . . . wub . . . wub . . . blop!

With a crash, cringle, pop and a wub, wub, blop, Buzz the Space Bus sat on the launch pad feeling very sorry for himself.

'What's up Buzz?' asked Valentina the Rescue Ship.

'Ooo, err, I don't know,' groaned Buzz, 'I feel sort of ooo, eerr whir, whir pop. My insides are all wrong and I can't blast off.'

Just then, an angry voice boomed out over the spaceport loudspeakers, 'Buzz the Space Bus. Will you please blast off. Your passengers are waiting on the moon. Here is your final countdown.
5 4 3 2 1 . . .'

But nothing happened, all Buzz did was to sit on the launch pad and feel sorry for himself.

'Now we're for it,' said Valentina. 'Now we're in big trouble.'

Mars

Out in space, Helen was well on her way to Mars carrying her load of ice-cream. The people on Mars had waited a long time for their favourite dessert and they'd all placed special orders – chocolate chip flavour, fish and chip flavour, and strawberry and straw flavour (which was for Viking – the Martian donkey).

Helen was singing happily to herself as she swung into orbit around Mars:

'Nice ice cream,

Helen has a dream,

To make the Martian people glad,

With the best dessert they've ever had.'

With that she slowed down and started to drop gently towards Mars, singing as she went.

Earth

Back on earth, Buzz was in a terrible state. The engineers had his boosters in pieces all over the launch pad.

'Ooo, er, please,' said Buzz. 'Do be careful with that screwdriver. I'm not just space junk you know.'

'You might as well be,' said Valentina. 'A rocket that's stuck on Earth is about as much use as a space helmet made out of jelly,' she laughed.

Buzz didn't laugh, he just said, 'Boo hoo', then 'Ouch, ow, stop that' as the engineers started to hammer at his rocket nozzles to shake out any loose bits that might be causing a blockage.

Mars

On Mars, Helen had just landed and was singing another song:

'Ice-cream, lovely ice-cream

Come and get your ice-cream

It'll make you cold,

It'll make you smile

It's yellow, blue and white and green.'

All the Martian people were rushing to the ice-cream landing site, all thinking of the delicious flavours that awaited them – Pizza Surprise (wouldn't you be surprised at Pizza-flavoured ice-cream?), Yam and Jam, Coconut and Yorkshire pudding, Apple and Whizzlenut Sundae (and if you don't know what that is, then it just proves that you've never lived on Mars).

Then came the big moment, Helen's doors were flung open and out came a huge river! It flowed round and round, pouring out of the cargo doors. It seemed to go on and on for ever. It appeared, in the Martian sunlight, to be made of all colours at once – swirling, surging, gushing and twisting with the colours mixing and flowing together. It looked wonderful, extraordinary, tremendous.

'Oh, dear,' said Helen. 'It looks like the ice-cream has melted and the flavours are all mixed in together. I was very careful on the flight from Earth, really I was.'

The Martian people weren't very upset about the flavours all being mixed up. As long as they had some ice-cream they didn't care.

So they all dived in to taste the mysterious mixture before it drained away into the Martian soil.

And did they think it was delicious?

NO THEY DID NOT.

'Yueck', said one.

'Ergghhh', said another.

But most just pulled a very horrible face and doubled up as if they'd been punched in the stomach. Until one Martian said, 'rocket fuel!'

Earth

And at that very moment on earth, an engineer turned on a tap to check Buzz's fuel and out of his fuel tanks came . . .

You guessed it.

ICE-CREAM.

Litres and litres of melted ice-cream in every flavour you could name and quite a few that you couldn't.

'Oh, that does feel better,' said Buzz. 'My tanks are so much easier now.'

'Someone filled you up with ice-cream instead of rocket fuel and it melted in the hot sun,' explained Valentina. 'No wonder you felt all wrong. Perhaps the engineers can explain how it happened?'

But for some reason the engineers were all down on their hands and knees. Perhaps they were just hiding their red faces because they'd given Buzz's fuel to Helen and put Helen's ice-cream in Buzz's fuel tanks. Whatever they were thinking, they were making very happy slurping noises!

Mars

There weren't any happy noises on Mars. Not that day. But a few days later, Valentina the Rescue Ship arrived with a new load of ice-cream, and a few days after that Buzz arrived with a bus load of Ice-Cream Technicians who showed the Martian people how to make their own ice-cream. Then, when the first tub of Martian ice-cream rolled off the production line, Yuri the Silver Rocket zoomed into orbit around Mars and did a few somersaults for everyone to see.

But, of course, no one was looking. They were all too busy eating ice-cream.

ACTIVITY 2 Talking about feelings DISCUSSING DIFFICULT FEELINGS

WHERE? All together in the story corner or in smaller groups as appropriate.

HOW? Story 1, *The Ice-cream Delivery*, introduced some of the 'Rocket' characters. Story 2, *Space Race*, is designed to use these characters and some new ones to a deeper purpose. Its light-hearted approach and simple characterisations provide a sense of 'distance', allowing the children to talk freely about characters' strong and difficult feelings in a situation far away from, yet similar to, their own.

NB: The new characters are Gigantica, Molly, Luna, and Wanda the Weather Satellite.

◆ *Tips for. . .* handling discussion of children's feelings

A story such as this can create an alternative world in which children can feel safe to discuss difficult emotions and can develop an appropriate vocabulary to talk about feelings in a non-threatening environment. Even so, any such work opens up the possibility that deep-seated emotions, perhaps due to family break-ups or other distressing events, will surface.

How such situations are dealt with will depend on a range of personal and situational factors applying to the individual child, the teacher, the school and the wider environment. One decision that any teacher faces in such circumstances is how much to allow the child to say in front of the rest of the class. A judgement will have to be made about the extent to which what is being said is of general interest and value, and at what point it becomes too personal to be handled within the class.

If you feel that such a point has been reached, you need to consider:

■ gently moving the discussion on

■ talking separately with the distressed child

■ dealing with the matter through the normal channels including the Headteacher, parents, psychologist and other support services.

Although detailed discussion of such pastoral arrangements are beyond the scope of this book, we would make a plea for the usefulness of feelings-related work in developing pupils' Speaking and Listening skills. Talking about real feelings will give pupils access to one of the richest seams of experience within them. Properly structured and with appropriate support, the majority of children will respond well to the ideas suggested here. The possibility that difficult situations may arise is testament to the importance of emotions in young lives. The ability to express joy and happiness adequately as well as anger, jealousy and sadness is an essential element in personal and social health.

The story features five strong emotions.

■ excitement – the general excitement and atmosphere of the race, and Yuri's specific excitement in Part 1

■ jealousy – as Yuri looks at all the other craft in Part 2

■ sadness – as Yuri considers his position in Part 3

- anger – as Luna feels cheated in Part 4
- happiness – when it all works out in the end!

As you tell the story you can focus on the feelings of the characters, by stopping at the end of each section and asking the children to recap on what has happened, and drawing them out on what each character is thinking and feeling at that particular time.

Alternatively you could recap and focus on feelings scene by scene after you have told the whole story.

Once you are sure that most children are clear on the characters and what happened in the story, you could use the feelings as the stimulus for re-telling all or parts of the story:

- Why was Yuri excited?
- Why was he jealous?
- What made Yuri sad?
- Who became angry at the end of the story?
- And why were Luna and Yuri happy in the end?

Now moving on from the story, give children the opportunity to talk about their own feelings of excitement, jealousy, sadness, anger or happiness (or any other emotion which is touched on as you talk about the story). Many children will recognise, for example, the kind of foot-stamping anger and sense of unfairness which Luna feels.

Develop this into asking the children what they would say to Yuri when he is sad, jealous, etc. This will work best if a specific outcome is looked for, for example asking 'What would you say to Yuri to cheer him up, to stop him feeling so down in the dumps about the race?'

Record some of the children's comments about feelings on a chart. We give four categories of feeling below, but a simpler version with just the one or two feelings to which the children readily responded would be just as effective.

Feelings

Excited
Yuri was excited at the space race.

We're all excited about our assembly.

Ms Hughes was excited when she learnt to cycle.

David is excited about his new rabbit.

Sad
Yuri was sad when he thought he wouldn't win.

We were sad when Mrs. Patel left.

Ms Hughes is sad when the big ones go up.

Michelle was sad when her goldfish died.

Angry
Luna was angry when she couldn't finish.

We were angry when a window was broken.

Ms Hughes is angry when we won't listen

Gabrielle is angry about the rain forest being cut down.

Happy
Luna and Yuri were happy at the end.

We're happy when we sing.

Ms Hughes is happy with our work.

Julie is happy when she has pizza for tea.

Choose one of the feelings with which your class has identified and brainstorm words relating to that feeling. Take any suggestions, even if you cannot see the connection at this stage – if chocolate ice-cream makes a child angry, so be it!

This needn't be a one-off activity. If you set up a 'feelings word bank' in one corner of the classroom, then whenever feelings come up in a story, poem, song, or even a real life situation, any pertinent words can be added to the list. You can add extra fun to this if the word bank is a cardboard box 'computer' with a slot in the top. Give the computer a name and explain that 'Chip' needs to know all about feelings, which is why you must feed in feeling words every so often. When you have a good collection of words, children can help 'Chip' by sorting the words into different lists depending on which feelings they relate to.

Feelings Word Lists

Happy	Angry	Sad	Excited
fun	stamp	cry	hooray
funny	shout	weep	keen
laugh	cross	tearful	can't wait
smile	mad	unhappy	yippee!
joke	annoyed	down	lively
whoopee!	tight inside	fed up	Christmas
friends	fist	miserable	presents
joy	smash	sorry	parties

Resource 10

Space Race

Part 1

5 4 3 2 1 Blast off.

'Whoopee,' shouted Yuri the Silver Rocket as he sped into the sky. Huge orange and red flames came shooting out of his boosters and a great stream of white smoke, like billowing clouds, trailed along behind.

Yuri was even more excited than usual because this was the day of the Round the Moon Space Race and he had been chosen from all the Spaceport rockets to try to win the gold medal for the Earth.

'Yuri's going to win, the rest go in the bin,' Yuri sang to himself as he swung in to orbit Earth.

Part 2

There were four rockets in the race: Yuri from the Earth, Gigantica from Jupiter, Molly from Mars and Luna from the Moon.

The others were already at the starting point as Yuri arrived in Earth orbit and fired his retros to slow down to a perfect stop at the official starting line just behind Wanda the Weather Satellite.

'You're here at last I see Yuri,' said Wanda in her strictest voice. 'Get into line quickly. The race starts shortly and besides, as soon as I've seen you lot off, I'm hitching a lift on Buzz the Space Bus. It's time for my check up on Earth.'

Yuri did as he was told, and as he manoeuvred into position, he stole a quick glance at the other rockets.

As soon as he looked at Gigantica, he felt a mighty surge in his circuits, a shock that was almost enough to fire his retro rockets and send him straight back to Earth. Gigantica had twenty-four giant rockets – enough to boost him to Pluto and back without stopping!

'Oh no, he's bound to win,' thought Yuri jealously. But then he looked at Molly and his heart sank even further. Molly was a shiny black, super smooth shape. She was right up-to-date and her single rocket engine looked like the most powerful that Yuri had ever seen.

Then Yuri saw Luna. Luna spent all her life going between the Earth and the Moon. She was a funny looking rocket, with giant solar panels like wings for collecting sunlight and turning it into extra power. She had bits sticking out in all directions – aerials, radar dishes, steering engines. She never landed on a planet, so she didn't need a smooth streamlined shape. She was built to do the journey between the Earth and the Moon as quickly as possible and even now she was straining forward as if she couldn't wait to start. Yuri wished that he felt like that.

Part 3

Poor Yuri! All his excitement had vanished into thin space.

'I'm going to lose,' he moaned, 'I just know I am.'

'Take your starting positions please,' announced Molly. 'Stand by. Ready, steady. Go!'

All the rockets roared into life. Yuri did his best but within seconds he was left behind as the three modern rockets with their giant engines and solar panels sped off towards the Moon.

'Goodbye Yuri!' said Gigantica over the space radio.

'So long, slow coach!' added Molly.

And just for good measure, Luna came on the line with one of her sing-song lunar rhymes:

'Yuri, you're in last place.

You won't win the Space Race.'

'Grr,' said Yuri, 'I'll show you.' But he didn't have the energy to say anything else as he tried to wring the last atom of extra power out of his straining engines.

Gigantica was in the lead, his rockets blazing away like a firework display. In second place and catching up with Gigantica was Molly, with Luna close behind her. Yuri was a long way behind but from where he was it seemed as though Luna was slowing down. Yuri couldn't resist teasing her on the space radio.

'What's the matter Luna?' taunted Yuri. 'I knew you couldn't keep up that speed. Are your fuel tanks running out already?'

But all that Luna said was, 'You'll see!'

Part 4

Yuri did see. He saw how Luna, who did this trip every day, slowed down to go around the Moon whereas Gigantica and Molly just kept going. They were speeding along and moving much too fast to go round the Moon. They just kept going in a straight line!

'Help!' cried Gigantica.

'Can't stop!' shouted Molly as the two rockets went hurtling off into outer space leaving the Moon and the race far behind.

'Good riddance to those two,' said Luna.

'Now its just me and you, Yuri. I'd like some company on the way back. Let me slow down for you.'

So that's how they travelled back, Luna giving her engines just enough power to keep ahead while Yuri had to go flat out to keep up.

It was obvious who was going to win, but, thought Yuri, 'At least I won't be last. In fact I'm bound to be second!'

When they reached the Earth, Yuri was puffing and panting away while Luna had power to spare. She made up another 'Luna Rhyme'.

'I'm Luna the moon ship

I don't like to boast

But I'll be first at the finishing . . . '

Finishing post? But where was the finishing post?

The race was due to end where it started, by Wanda the Weather Satellite. But she was nowhere to be seen.

'Where's the finishing post?' shouted Luna. 'I demand to win the race.'

Part 5

Suddenly with a click and whir of his computer, Yuri remembered.

'Wanda's gone down to Earth on Buzz the Space Bus, don't you remember? And since the race must finish where it started and since you're not built to land on a planet, I think that makes me the winner. Goodbye.'

And he fired his retro rockets and made a neat landing on Earth right next to where Wanda sat on the Spaceport runway.

'But that's not . . . that's not . . . it's just not fair,' spluttered Luna as she circled the Earth getting crosser and crosser.

Yuri got his medal but not the one he expected. It was decided that Luna was the real winner of the race. After all it wasn't her fault that the winning post had moved to the Earth. Luna was very pleased with this, but Yuri was happy too because his medal was a special one. It said: 'For Yuri the Silver Rocket. Awarded to the earth for, entering the race, trying his hardest and the cheekiest win ever.'

◆ *Tips for. . .* story-telling

Teachers are the unsung heroes of story-telling. Every day in thousands of classrooms stories are told and read, even acted by teachers of all ages, experience and backgrounds. The art of story-telling spans cultures and races, and embraces a tremendous range of styles. Any tips suggested here will probably serve only to express those things which many teachers do instinctively and have learnt through the most valuable experience, namely regular story-telling to the most discerning of audiences. All this in the midst of a busy day with a thousand other things to think about and with classroom management and control strategies never out of mind! Small wonder that teachers soon learn to tell stories effectively and to adapt material to their own needs and those of their children.

■ Try to read the material beforehand and, if possible, mark any words which will need extra stress, or places where a change of voice or mood is appropriate.

■ If you can find the time to practise out loud you'll find that the shape and structure of the story is much easier to appreciate. We read so quickly compared with reading aloud that it's hard to appreciate the vocal effect of a word, phrase or sentence until we actually speak it. Reading the story to one or two children can be a good way to identify potentially confusing elements before trying it out on a class.

■ Think about your use of space beforehand. In a story with two locations, simply moving from one side of the board or one chair to another can be tremendously helpful to children who are trying to make sense of the story. Even a simple movement such as shifting position as you sit can be effective – for a burrowing mole you lean forward, for a proud fox you sit upright. As mentioned above, you will probably do these things instinctively but it can be useful to think them through in advance.

■ Think about your use of voice. There will be a considerable variation in style and ability here, with some teachers giving virtuoso solo performances complete with character voices and appropriate gestures whilst others will prefer a cooler approach which allows the words alone to paint the picture. Whatever your approach, and there's a good chance it'll fall somewhere between the extremes, give some thought to the most helpful way of using your voice when speaking the words of characters in the story. A good starting point is to aim for clarity, asking yourself, 'If I didn't say "said Helen", or "shouted Yuri", would the children know which character was speaking by my tone and style of voice?'

■ Use simple props. Wearing a shawl can create an air of mystery and clearly show that you're shifting into story-telling mode. This might be appropriate for a legend or any story with a sense of long ago and far away.

You can use a number of props to represent different characters, holding them when appropriate. There's a danger here that once three or more characters appear together you run out of hands and spend more time concentrating on props than on the story! You could place the props in front of you and point to them occasionally as reminders, or you could use pictures which the children draw in advance and walk along your display, stopping at the appropriate point.

■ Teachers often allow children to interact with the story as they read, using such strategies as:

– stopping to talk about difficult words

– allowing children to join in with repeated phrases or sound effects

– predicting what will happen

– recalling the story so far

– discussing events or characters in the story

– relating the story theme to the children's own experiences.

These discussions often arise spontaneously but it can be useful to plan stopping points in advance, particularly in a long or difficult story.

■ Use illustrations as part of the above interaction, particularly when recalling the story so far, setting the scene, picking up again after a gap, or when predicting what may happen. The danger of using illustrations in this way is that they can influence the children's own mind pictures and prevent them from forming their own imaginative characters and settings (much as fans of *The Archers* complain when they see the actors in the flesh!), so there may be times when you wish to use illustrations sparingly or allow the children to provide the pictures. One variant of this approach is to ask the children to work in small groups to create illustrations for the story in the form of 'still pictures'.

ACTIVITY 3 Feelings dance

EXPRESSING FEELINGS THROUGH SOUND AND MOVEMENT

WHERE?   There is a range of ideas – physical location will depend on which you choose to use.

HOW?   The aim is to create a 'Feelings Dance' using movement and sound.

You can create feelings in sound, using percussion instruments:

■ heavy bangs and thuds for anger

■ tinkling cymbals and glockenspiel for excitement

■ rumbles and sharp clashes for anger

■ harmonious sounds for happiness, and so on.

You can also use appropriate recorded music to inspire the dance – the well known *Tubular Bells* by Mike Oldfield offers themes that can accompany 'Anger', 'Excitement' and 'Happiness'.

Children might be happy to develop their own ideas and structure for the dance. Alternatively you could use the more definite structure outlined in the 'Feelings Dance' sheet on page 88.

You could use music and sound only. Or, you could narrate the story in the left-hand column while the children enact it.

It should be stressed that the 'Feelings Dance' sheet offers guidance for a movement session – it is not meant for performance to a separate audience. The mime would be hard for an audience to follow. However, performance is an important aspect of the P.E. National Curriculum and you may take the opportunity to allow children to view and comment upon each other's work as the dance progresses.

Resource 11

Feelings Dance

ACTION	GROUPS	FEELING	DANCE QUALITY
Children waking up, getting out of bed, rubbing eyes, stretching, etc.	Solo	Slow, gentle start	Slow, stretching
Opening curtains, shielding eyes from bright sun, getting dressed enthusiastically.		Happiness	Sharper movements
Look around for sock. Can't find it, get increasingly cross. Stamp around. Shout and scream. (mime!)		Anger	Exaggerated physical expression of mood
Spot sock in other 'bedroom', try to grab it from partner, tug of war with (imaginary) sock.	Now form into pairs		Travelling
One wins and puts sock on, the other produces box (mimed present). Shields it from other partner who looks on jealously.		Jealousy	Mimetic dance
Partner with box starts to undo it. There are many wrappings and boxes within boxes. Eventually the centre is reached. The one with the parcel holds up its contents. One sock!	Pairs		Comic, large gestures
They both laugh and roll around with laughter. The sock is put on and they sit down together.		Happiness	Exaggerated mime and bringing dance to a clear end

Development across Key Stages 1 and 2...

If the 'Rockets' characters capture your class's imagination, there are a number of ways in which this could be developed.

Design and Technology   Children could:

■ draw or paint the rockets

■ design their own rocket and give it a name

■ draw their own ice-cream tub showing a special Martian flavour

■ make a model of the spaceport out of boxes, etc.

Writing and Speech   Children could:

■ write, illustrate, and read out a postcard from Mars saying how hungry they are for ice-cream

■ design a rocket (as above), and talk through their design, telling the rest of the class what the rocket is called and what it does

■ write or tell another adventure for one of the rockets

■ talk as a whole class about their favourite ice-cream and make up some new flavours

■ with the whole class, write a new song for Helen about the day she took rocket fuel to Mars by mistake

■ write a space poem using some of the words from the story, such as 54321 Blast off, Whoosh!, Zoom, gigantic roar, Martian, meteorite, rocket fuel, orbit.

Science

■ look at the position of Mars in the Solar System

■ tell the stories of the real Yuri (Gagarin – first man in space), Valentina (Tereshkova – first woman in space), Buzz (Aldrin – Apollo 11) and Helen (Sharman – Britain's first astronaut). Use these stories to discuss gravity and weightlessness.

■ conduct a 'blind tasting' of different ice-cream flavours!

Underground

Curriculum context

Essentially this is an English task in which children develop a verbal vocabulary to describe life underground. It uses dance, however, to encourage them to develop their descriptions of an underground world, and leads to a dance performance.

The task is linked to the Science curriculum throughout – but particularly in Activity 1 with the classification of objects.

Key Strategy

In the Dragons unit children worked together to create a class poem using sound effects. In these activities we use dance in a similar way – to intensify and enrich children's language. The ultimate aim is to create an unusual class performance combining evocative language and movement.

Expected outcomes

■ imaginative work linking movement and language

■ the opportunity to develop and participate in a performance

■ focused listening as children listen for and act on a given cue.

How to use the material

The performance could be prepared over a number of sessions. Make sure that children are given time to recall their 'underground' words before Activity 2 and their dance before attempting Activity 3.

You will need

■ Recorded music – e.g. Tomita, *Snowflakes are Dancing* (album): track 'The Engulfed Cathedral'; *The Elemental Wizard* effects and music tape, published by BBC Educational Publications, BBC White City, London W30 7TS; Holst, *The Planets* (*Saturn*).

ACTIVITY 1 Underground words

WHERE? In the story corner or seated at tables, which ever is best for class brainstorming!

HOW? This is a simple brainstorming exercise in which the children share their ideas and knowledge about things that are underground.

A good way to record this is to have a large sheet of paper as below. As children offer their ideas the class place them into one of the two categories.

You could further develop this into Maths-based work on sets if you think it is appropriate.

UNDERGROUND

LIVING THINGS

WORMS
RABBITS
MOLES
ANTS
BADGERS

OTHER THINGS

TUNNELS
PIPES
WIRES
STONES
DIGGING MACHINES

ACTIVITY 2 Underground dance

WHERE? In the hall or cleared classroom space.

HOW? Ask the children to find their own space and to think for a moment of all the underground things that they have talked about. Prompt them with suggestions from the brainstorm list if necessary.

Explain that you want the children to choose one underground thing and to pretend to be that thing when the music starts. It can be something that moves around like an animal or a digging machine, or it might be something still like a water pipe, or it could be the water rushing through the pipe. The idea is to portray as wide a range of underground things as possible.

Choose a piece of music that gives a sense of mystery and strangeness and which encourages slow, pushing movements, although this may not be entirely appropriate for every child's chosen movement. A good example would be 'The Engulfed Cathedral' from the album *Snowflakes are Dancing* by Tomita. This is a synthesised version of Debussy's Tone Poems and has the right kind of qualities including a watery feel which might also be appropriate.

You may also like to use a tambourine or other percussion instrument so that you can fit the sounds to the children's ideas.

Allow the children a little time to develop their own dance ideas, then you could split the class into two halves and allow each half to watch the other's dance.

In order to add detail and depth to the children's movement, look at factors such as:

■ the sense of tension and power as creatures push through the earth

■ the body shapes they make

■ have they moved from simple mime into more extended movements?

■ do they look interesting?

■ do they give the 'right idea'?

Encourage them to see movement as a physical language – with each body posture or movement having a precise meaning within this dance. Is there one dance that seems particularly appropriate to convey a word or phrase?

Do not overdo the analysis of the dance, however. You should stop while the children are still enjoying it, whilst it is fresh and stimulating, and not go through too many refinements. The children should be familar enough with the theme and their own dance to be able to use them in a different way to respond to the narration in the next section.

ACTIVITY 3 Combining underground words and dance

WHERE? In the same space as for Activity 2.

HOW? The idea here is to combine the children's words and dances, using the narration on page 94 (preferably read by the teacher) with children responding on cue.

The exact method of working on this, of rehearsing and trying out ideas, will vary from teacher to teacher. We offer one model below:

1. Read through the narration to the children and spend a short while discussing each paragraph: what is its focus? what is the rhythm and feel of it? what feelings do the words evoke? Explain any words that children might find difficult.

2. Adapt the narration to include the children's own suggestions. They could draw on their underground words and phrases from Activity 1. Our narration is only a loose structure into which other words and phrases can easily be fitted or substituted.

3. The class can work in three groups – each performs their movement with one paragraph of narration. Alternatively all children can be involved in all the dance. Either way once the narration is finalised, highlight a key phrase in each paragraph for children to listen for as their cue.

4. Explain what dance sequence they are expected to do on their cue.

5. Try out the words along with the children's dances and sort out any practical difficulties such as children unsure of when to move (in which case they can follow another child who has picked up the cue), or children whose dance paths collide!

6. Talk the children into the situation by stressing the atmosphere and type of movement required, before trying again.

7. If appropriate, end this session by adding music to the dance and narration from the teacher.

Resource 12

NARRATION	ACTION
It is dark underground. It is quiet underground. But there are things underground, things made by people underground. Hundreds of tiny wires for telephones. Pipes for water. Pipes for gas. Tunnels for trains. Underground, under your feet, under, under, underground.	*Children curled up like rocks about the space.* *Some children make pipe and wire shapes, perhaps moving to join together.*
It is dark underground. It is quiet underground. But there are things underground. Animals and insects hurrying and scurrying. Tiny ants. A digging mole. And worms squirm around, under, under, underground.	*As the various animals are mentioned they uncurl and move appropriately around the space, in and out of the 'pipe and wire' children.*
It is dark underground. It is quiet underground. But there are people underground. People in trains rushing through tunnels. People digging, making the tunnels. People at work deep underground, under, under, underground.	*Other children (or could be the 'pipe and wire' children changing role) sit like a group of people on a train and/or mime digging a tunnel.* *All freeze for final 'Underground Tableau'.*

Development across Key Stages 1 and 2 . . .

DEVELOPING A PERFORMANCE

This performance piece could be combined with work from the Dragons unit for a more ambitious performance, perhaps for an assembly or as a play for parents, along the following lines:

1. Children move to starting positions.

2. Teacher introduces work on underground theme.

3. Class perform the dance as in Activity 3. After each paragraph of narration the music swells and the dance continues until the teacher begins to read the next verse.

4. Children gather around teacher.

5. Teacher invites those watching to close their eyes and imagine that they are underground.

6. Children perform a conducted montage of underground sounds (see Dragons page 41 for suggestions on this).

7. Teacher introduces the class's 'Dragon Poem', explaining that the class have been thinking about one particular creature that might live underground.

8. Teacher and children perform their 'Dragon Poem'.

DEVELOPING OTHER TYPES OF DANCE

We have investigated the world of 'underground' in this dance session. Pupils could equally well work on 'underwater' or 'in mid air' – to broaden the range of dance and language requirements.

They could use their imaginations to create words and movements to go with less familiar worlds such as 'another planet', or 'moon landscape' or 'polar landscape'.

Pupils could imagine a scenario in which they have shrunk to a tiny size and, although they are in their normal world, everything now seems changed – how could words and dance convey this?

There are many further suggestions and support for Dance work in The weekly Key Stage 2 series *Dance Workshop* from School Radio. For younger children, *Let's Move* and *Time to Move* offer similar ideas.

STRATEGIES AND ACTIVITIES FOR Y3/Y4

Christmas

Curriculum context

This is a set of drama activities to use in exploring the Christmas story. It can be used particularly in the context of an RE topic on festivals or as part of the school Christmas celebrations. There are also links to History and PSHE.

Key Strategies

A range of drama strategies are employed, including 'still pictures', 'living pictures', teacher in role and 'speaking thoughts'.

Pupils are encouraged to improvise.

Expected outcomes

- a greater knowledge of the Christmas story
- increased confidence in speaking in group situations
- increased ability to talk in role.

How to use the material

It's Christmas again! You might be looking for yet another new angle on a well-told story, or you might be in a school where the story is less well known.

In either case the drama ideas suggested in this unit are designed to help children to recall or to find out about the story and to focus on two of the most accessible aspects of the story: the desperate search for somewhere to have the baby, and the celebration of the birth.

The drama activities should work well used in full and in the order we suggest, but each one can also be used independently in a variety of ways and, as you will see from later activities in this book, to look at a range of themes, issues and stories.

You will need

- props for teacher in role.

ACTIVITY 1 **Christmas**

WHERE? In the hall or cleared classroom space or anywhere with enough room for active group work.

HOW? Using 'Christmas' as the key word, ask children to work in groups to make 'still pictures' which show some aspect of the festival. At this stage it can be anything that children respond to: presents, Father Christmas, parties, etc.

◆ *Tips for . . .* **making still pictures**

- The bigger the group, the more organisation is needed. Still pictures work well in groups of two, three or four.

- You will have your own policy on the formation of groups, but this might be a good opportunity to select mixed sex working groups and to take account of the fact that ability in this kind of work needn't correspond to academic ability.

- Encourage children to get up and try out ideas soon and not to talk for too long.

- If children are new to still pictures, you might find that their images are indistinct – they know what they're doing but to an observer it just looks like children standing around. Encourage them to think about showing some people in different positions and to make the picture as clear as possible.

- Three to five minutes should be long enough for the working out of the pictures, at which point you can give a countdown from five to one and on 'one' ask each group to freeze in their picture. You can then make a few general comments and allow 'one more minute' before the pictures are shared with the rest of the class.

- There are a number of ways that the pictures can be shared:

  - the whole class freezes and you ask everyone to look around the room from their frozen position.

  - a variation of the above is that once everyone has seen the pictures you bring them to life for a few moments before freezing again.

  - ask half the class to sit down while the other half show their pictures, then swap over. You can use this to make a comment on each group and allow the watchers to ask questions. You can also start the sharing by going round to each group in turn and asking the watchers, 'What's happening in this picture?'

  - see the groups one by one, again with questions and comments. The disadvantage of this is that it can take quite a while, and the watchers may get restless.

Activity 2 The Christmas story

WHERE? Continuing in the same place as Activity 1.

HOW? For this section, children will need to have some knowledge of the Christmas story and the main characters in it. You could break after Activity 1 and gather the children around, asking them about the story and filling in the gaps so they are ready for the 'instant pictures'. Alternatively, you could build the session into continuing curriculum work around the Christmas story.

'Instant pictures' are a form of 'still pictures' where the children work individually and respond instantly to your key word or phrase. This is the same technique as used in the Long Ago unit (page 68). Announce the phrase which they need to turn into a picture then, on a given signal, they make up their picture.

Spread the children out around the space. Choose phrases which relate to people and events in the story such as:

- Mary or Joseph on the journey
- the wise men follow the star
- the shepherds look after their sheep
- Mary and Joseph look for somewhere to stay
- the angel appears to the shepherds
- the baby is born.

Now you are going to add a talk element. Allow children to choose a moment from the story freely and to form an instant picture of it. It could be either something they have already done or something new.

On your signal, children form and hold their picture. When the pictures are formed, you go round and touch individuals on the shoulder. This is their signal for them to say who they are and what they are doing: 'I'm a wise man following the star', 'I'm a shepherd looking after my sheep', etc.

ACTIVITY 3 **The Bethlehem market-place**   LIVING PICTURES

WHERE?   As in Activities 1 and 2, in a hall or cleared space.

HOW?   Now that the story should be fairly well fixed in the children's minds, call them together and explain the next stage of the drama in which they are all going to become people in the market in Bethlehem.

The first stage of this is to establish a common idea of what a market is and the sort of things that would happen in such a market.

You'll need to make fine judgements about how important historical accuracy is, perhaps finding it important to explain why they can't have a stall selling videos, for example. On the other hand, it would not be helpful to overburden the children with historical information which might prevent them from entering into the drama fully.

The narration suggested below might help. As you talk with the class, let them build up a picture of the market and their place within it.

■ Will they be buyers or sellers?

■ What will they sell? Clothes, sandals, fruit, bread, wooden carvings, leather goods?

■ What have they come to buy?

The important point is to establish the mood and feel of a busy, lively market.

Ask the children to find their starting position, then read out this scene-setting narration (or your own adaptation of it):

It's very early in the morning, so early that the hot sun is only just rising. But it's time for you to wake up. Turn over in your sleep and start to wake up.

Quickly get dressed.

Now drink your cup of goat's milk and eat a piece of bread.

It's time to get ready for the market. What will you take with you today?

If you're buying, you'll need to find your money and a bag to carry things, and you'll need to think about what you'll be buying.

If you're selling, you'll need to collect together all your things and either carry them or load up your camel.

Now off you go to market. If you see anyone else on the journey, give them a friendly wave.

Now you've arrived at the market. If you're buying, sit down for a rest, have a drink from your water-bottle and count out your money.

If you're selling, you'd better set up your stall. Get everything out and display it ready for sale.

In a moment, the market begins. So buyers get up, sellers be ready and off you go . . .

Now the whole class enacts the market, with different stalls selling a variety of things and the buyers moving from stall to stall, buying, talking, perhaps complaining and so on.

Be prepared for this to be 'messy' and not focused at the first attempt and then stop after a few minutes in order to help the class get more out of it. You could:

■ encourage the buyers to have a clearer idea of what they want

■ let the sellers combine to work in groups of two, three or four

■ give the sellers the task of working out a simple chant or phrase to attract customers

■ introduce the idea of haggling over prices.

You could also stop the action every so often and ask most of the class to watch one small area (one or two stalls and their customers) for a few moments in order to learn from one another.

Finally stop the action and sit the children down as you explain what is going to happen next.

ACTIVITY 4 **Searching for a room**

WHERE?   Continuing from Activity 3 above.

HOW?   Recap on the fact that the town is crowded (and why, if necessary).

Explain that you are now going to be joining in the action. You are going to be someone who is looking for a room because you or your wife are going to have a baby very soon. You will be coming to the market asking if anyone knows of a room.

In order to differentiate your new role from your 'teacher role' you could put on a simple shawl or wrap to indicate when you are 'in role'.

If appropriate, you could ask a child to accompany you, or even ask two children to take on the Mary and Joseph roles while you remain outside the drama.

Start up the market activity as before and then join in as the person looking for a room.

If children tell you that they do know of a room, you can go off to investigate, only to return saying that there was no space after all.

It may be that children offer to let you come and live with them! You could choose to do so, and thus take the drama off in a new direction. You could stop the drama and explore reasons why that might not be practical, or you could find a reason from within the drama ('I need somewhere nearer', 'You're very kind but I think we should stay in an inn', etc).

There are further tips for handling 'Teacher in Role' on page 133.

If appropriate, end this section of the drama with there being nowhere for you to stay. Or, if you have found somewhere to stay, introduce the idea that in the Bible story there was no room anywhere.

ACTIVITY 5 **Nowhere to stay**

WHERE? All sitting in a circle.

HOW? Gather the class around you in a circle and ask them to imagine how 'you' feel and to be ready to speak 'your' thoughts.

You could remain in the middle of the circle in a dejected pose for this, or if you need to be outside the drama at this point, for control or organisational reasons, you could use a child in your place at the centre of the circle, or take off the shawl that you wore as the person seeking shelter, and place this in the middle to represent your role.

Simply allow the children to take it in turns around the circle to speak one word or simple phrase which expresses the thoughts and feelings of the shelter seeker. Allow children to pass or to repeat what has been said already, so as not to turn what should be a reflective exercise into a performance.

You might wish to record the words spoken at this point (either on paper or tape), for later use in Christmas poems, prose or perhaps a school Christmas play.

ACTIVITY 6 The birth of the baby

WHERE? Sitting in a circle as in Activity 5.

HOW? Sit the class down and recap the end of the story – the birth of Jesus in a stable.

Taking suggestions from the class as to the best pose and position, model this part of the story using children to form a 'still picture' in the centre of the circle. You could use just one or two children as if they are the parent(s) with the baby. Other children could be added as:

■ the stable (a simple arch made by two children can be very effective)

■ animals

■ wise men

■ shepherds

■ angels.

Then repeat the 'speaking thoughts' exercise, this time with the emphasis on the good news of the birth of a child. If all the children are in the picture, then touch individuals on the shoulder as a cue for them to speak their thoughts; if some remain in the circle you can go round one by one as before.

Try to keep the sense of reality that you will have established in the drama, so that the children's picture and words grow out of their drama experience of the situation, its tensions and difficulties, rather than being influenced by a 'Christmas card' approach. It might be that, for this reason, you choose to model only the parent(s), so keeping the focus on those most centrally involved.

Development across Key Stages 1 and 2 . . .

DRAMA STRATEGIES The strategies in this section are among the most flexible for use in Key Stages 1 and 2. They are the mainstay of much dramatic activity. You will find many other uses of these drama strategies in the context of History, Geography, RE and PSHE throughout this book.

Jealousy

STRUCTURED TALK, POETRY AND CHANTS

Curriculum context

These language-based activities are presented as if part of a PSHE programme in which pupils are helped to talk about, explore and deal with feelings of jealousy. There is also a link to Art in Activity 2.

Key Strategy

It is in the nature of Speaking and Listening that these skills will both develop from and lead into other kinds of work. In this section we show how different types of Speaking and Listening activity – whole class discussion, small group discussion, poetry, chants – can be intertwined with other writing and Art activities.

Expected outcomes

■ enhanced vocabulary

■ increased confidence in speaking about feelings

■ creative working as individuals, in small groups, and as a whole class

■ opportunity for discussion and exploring an issue of great relevance to the social health of any individual, class or community.

How to use the material

We present a range of approaches to exploring jealousy. The material does not require children to dig deeply into their own personal experience, although there is scope to develop the more personal side if this is appropriate.

We have not attempted to lead these activities into any overall conclusion as to what to do about jealous feelings. Rather we have attempted to highlight the power of jealousy.

You might find the material particularly useful if it is used alongside a book that the class is reading in which jealousy plays a part, e.g. *Ramona* by Beverley Cheery, or *Teddy Robinson* by Joan Robinson.

Or, it may simply be useful as a model for exploring emotions in talk and in written English.

You will need

■ copies of the short narrative in Activity 1

■ art materials for Activity 2.

ACTIVITY 1 **What is jealousy?**   WHOLE CLASS DISCUSSION

WHERE?   In the classroom or wherever class discussions take place.

HOW?   Start with the simple question 'What is Jealousy?'. Build a discussion around it. Ask children:

- to suggest words related to jealousy – distrust, envy, resentment, spite

- to look up and read out dictionary definitions of jealousy

- to look up and read out synonyms from a Thesaurus

- for examples from their experience

- to recall examples from books or films they have read or seen, such as:

  - Bill, who is jealous of the boys playing football in *Bill's New Frock* by Anne Fine

  - Jealousy related to the lamp in *Aladdin*

  - Edmund's jealousy of his sister in *The Lion, the Witch and the Wardrobe* by C.S. Lewis

  - Scarface's jealous possessiveness of the land in the *Animals of Farthing Wood*

  - Numerous examples from TV soaps!

Then move on to consider what jealousy feels like:

- Can children speak from personal experience?

- What kinds of words can be used to describe the experience of wanting something really badly, and resenting the fact that someone else has it?

If it helps, you can use the description on the resource sheet as a stimulus for discussion.

Talk about the way that the writer describes her jealousy, pulling out words and phrases such as:

- my stomach felt like a fist.

- it wasn't fair.

- . . . my neck was so solid I could hardly breathe.

- Inside, I felt all messy and churned up.

- I have to be that part.

- I just wish I was like her.

What difference does it make when the writer changes from talking about 'last night' to 'now'?

Can the children continue the story, say what happens next? How does the jealousy get dealt with, or does it just grow and grow?

I was angry with my friend
I told my wrath
My wrath did end.

I was angry with my foe
I told it not
My wrath did grow.

WILLIAM BLAKE

Does the same apply to jealousy? Should you tell someone that you are jealous of them?

Can jealousy be a good thing sometimes?

ACTIVITY 2 Images of jealousy SMALL GROUP ARTWORK

WHERE? In groups or individually at tables.

HOW? The idea is to create a class display around the theme of jealousy.

We recommend that children work in small groups discussing and experimenting with ways of translating a feeling into a picture. The kind of ideas they might consider are:

■ glossy pictures cut from magazines of the kinds of things that people aspire to – flashy cars, cameras, hi-fi, video, high fashion, the 'right' kind of trainers, make up, lush beaches

■ an attempt to depict a 'jealous-looking face'

■ an abstract swirl of colour, perhaps based on phrases such as: 'Inside, I felt all messy and churned up' and 'My stomach felt like a fist'.

When the images are ready, they can be mounted on a display board or wall, with space around them to add the results of the written work which follows.

ACTIVITY 3 Jealous words

WHERE? At tables.

HOW? Now set children the task of describing in a poem what it feels like to be jealous.

Start with a word list. A typical list might include: cross, unhappy, sad, want, tense, tight, confused, love, need . . .

Add phrases which give a sense of what it feels like to be jealous: mixed up, I've got to have it, want it now, can't think of anything else . . .

Choose a structure for the poem such as:

■ A poem where every line begins 'Jealousy is' .

■ A short, pithy poem that gives a real sense of what it feels like to be jealous. Use as few words as possible, perhaps starting with 'When you're jealous, you feel . . . '

■ Create shape poems, perhaps with the words swirling and spiralling, or forming a jealous-looking face.

■ Pupils might find it easier to create an expression of jealousy if they base the poem around a character. There is an example on the resource sheet.

Arrange the children's written work around the pictures to form a display which can also be used as a backdrop for Activity 4.

ACTIVITY 4 Chants

WHERE? In the classroom discussion area.

HOW? One aspect of jealousy is that we don't feel at all in control of our own feelings and this makes the use of simple repetitive chants an evocative way of conveying feelings of jealousy.

You could start simply with the word JEALOUSY and experiment with the class trying different ways of saying the word:

■ whispering, building to a climax, then receding

■ strongly rhythmic

■ with different groups/individuals following different rhythms, saying the word at varying levels and length

■ adding percussion – perhaps an 'irritating' repetitive rasp and occasional loud clashes at appropriate points.

Build a sound picture using more words taken from the class's discussions –

'envy', 'spite', 'I want', etc. Each word can be evaluated for the most appropriate way to deliver it – short and sharp for 'SPITE', a longer, more sinister delivery for 'I WANT', for example.

A vocal, musical poem of this type can be a lot of fun to work out and to practise. It requires a disciplined approach so that everyone comes in on cue, and watches for hand signals from the teacher.

This activity could be developed by adding some of the poems and prose extracts (including perhaps some from books as well as those written by the children). To do this, you first create a 'bed' of sound using the chants, over

which the other elements are added, as cued. If properly developed and rehearsed this could make an unusual contribution to an assembly or performance for parents.

Resource 13

I couldn't sleep at all last night. I tried and tried, but I couldn't put it out of my mind. I got up really early and my stomach felt like a fist. It was so tight, I thought if I saw her on the way to school, my stomach would jump out of its own accord and punch her. It wasn't fair. I knew what would happen after break, I just knew it.

During break my stomach got so tight that it started spreading right up my throat, till my neck was so solid I could hardly breathe. I knew that my voice was all wrong, all tense and cramped. Inside, I felt all messy and churned up.

Now it's after break and Miss has just said that this is the moment we've all been waiting for, when we will read the parts for the Christmas play. Suddenly, I don't want it to be Christmas, I don't want to go through the next hour, I only want to get the main part in the play. I have to be that part. I've thought of nothing else for days, but now that the time has come, I'd rather stay hoping that I could get it, than know that I haven't got it, know that Tanya – the best dancer, the best reader, the best actor, will be the main part, just like she was last year.

I don't hate Tanya, I just wish I was like her, I want to be the main part, I really, really want to get that part, but I just know I won't and that Tanya will.

He's got the latest trainers
    . . . and he makes sure everyone knows
His mum earns lots of money
    . . . and he makes sure everyone knows
He's always going on holiday
    . . . and he makes sure everyone knows
By sending them fancy postcards
    . . . from every place he goes.

His Walkman is the latest
    . . . and he makes sure everyone knows
His CD collection, the greatest
    . . . and it grows and grows and grows
He's always showing off his stuff
    . . . and he makes sure everyone knows
That he's so much better than you or me
    . . . and so is everything he owns.

UNIT 9

Hanuman   PUPPET STORY-TELLING AND DRAMA

Curriculum context

This series of activities is RE based, using part of the epic Hindu poem, the *Ramayana*, as a focus for story-telling and drama. In the puppet making activity there are links to Art, Craft and Design and Technology and, in the sound effects, links to Science. Whilst we have presented this work in an RE context there are other curriculum areas in which puppet work can be used.

Key Strategies

In these activities the puppets are used as an aid to develop children's speaking and story-telling skills.

Working with puppets can have an unexpectedly liberating effect on children. As the puppet draws the focus away from themselves it allows them to speak with confidence for, or on behalf of, their puppet character. This strategy can therefore be particularly effective for those children who otherwise lack confidence in speaking in front of others.

As a drama technique the other key strengths of working with puppets are:

■ a sense of fun, or of mystery, which can be a powerful stimulus

■ a sense of the theatrical – coming together to tell a story which young children respond to

■ puppets can perform any number of things which would be impossible for a human, and young children can achieve quite sophisticated results

■ puppets are easy to watch – they are simple and do not send confusing signals to the audience; their appearance gives some clue as to their nature.

Expected outcomes

■ familiarity with and enjoyment of a classic religious text

■ appropriate use of speech and sound effects for dramatic effect

■ increased confidence in speaking dramatic dialogue and telling a story

■ expressing emotions and feelings verbally

■ shared sense of involvement and creativity.

How to use the material

Activity 1 is designed to encourage familiarity with the story.

NB: A version of the Hanuman story which is accessible to young children is *The Amazing Adventures of Hanuman*, told by Rani and Jugnu Singh, with illustrations by Biman Mullick, published by BBC Books.

Activity 2 covers the making of the puppets.

Activity 3 covers the developing of the dialogue.

Activity 4 covers the presentation of a performance.

You will need

■ puppet-making equipment.

ACTIVITY 1 Getting to know Hanuman LISTENING TO A STORY

WHERE? In the classroom at tables.

HOW? Hanuman is a character from the epic Hindu poem the *Ramayana*.

This classic Indian legend is over 4,000 years old and is well known to Hindus all over the world. There are many gods and demigods, as well as humans and animals in the story. There is much magic, cunning, romance and adventure which makes it ideal for retelling using puppets.

Hanuman himself is a demigod, half monkey, half human. He is mischievous, magical, naughty and impetuous.

Before you start to tell the story you could introduce puppet versions of the characters (which you have made or which other children have created). Use this as an early focus on the characters before you introduce the story, revealing the characters one by one. Encourage the children to talk about the characters and who they think they are, what they might do, etc.

Here is one small episode in the story of Hanuman. You can flesh it out either from a published source or from your own knowledge of the story.

Hanuman is the son of Vayu, god of the winds, and his mother is a monkey princess.

Hanuman decides he would like to play with the Sun.

He reaches up into the sky, catches hold of the Sun and starts playing with it.

He treats the Sun as children would a ball – throwing it around the sky.

Indra, the god of thunder and lightning, is flying by on his magic elephant and he hears the Sun groaning and complaining at being thrown about.

Indra is cross with Hanuman and calls up a storm but Hanuman refuses to put the Sun down.

So Indra shoots a dart of lightning, at Hanuman. He is hit and falls to the ground.

Hanuman's father, Vayu, senses that his son is in danger and seeks him out.

The mighty storm is still blowing but, because of what has happened to his son, Vayu makes all the air stop moving on the Earth. Every living thing begins to suffer and die because of the lack of air.

Indra realises that all this has happened because he was angry with Hanuman.

He asks Vayu's forgiveness and breathes life back into Hanuman.

The Sun and Indra both give gifts of magical powers to Hanuman, and Vayu makes the air move on the Earth again, restoring everything to life.

ACTIVITY 2 Making puppets

WHERE?   In the classroom at 'making tables'.

HOW?   Children will need puppets of the four characters in the story:

■ **Hanuman**   The monkey boy. He could be depicted as a monkey, or perhaps a half human/half monkey combination.

■ **The Sun**   A simple disk or a sphere – brightly painted, with a face?

■ **Indra**   The god of thunder and lightning, a human shape, or perhaps a dark cloud with a face or a combination of cloud and lightning flashes? He wears a crown because he is a god.

■ **Vayu**   Hanuman's father, the god of the winds. A blowing cloud or a human form. He wears a crown to denote his deity.

There are any number of ways of making puppets:

■ The children can paint and decorate simple glove puppets.

■ A simple stick puppet can be made by drawing the character onto card stuck to a stick. The puppet can be operated from below in a Punch and Judy format, or from the side in a Pollock's Theatre style. For this most basic form you could simply copy, cut and mount the images on page 116.

■ More complex stick puppets can be made with moving limbs which are operated by sticks.

■ Shadow puppets can be very effective.

■ Large body puppets can be made by drawing round someone, colouring the character on the outline and cutting holes for eyes. After cutting it out the puppet arms can be attached to the children's arms and heads by a band of paper and the puppet is ready for use in a performance.

■ Marionettes are very difficult to make and liable to tangle so we do not recommend them. A very simple two-stringed puppet could, perhaps, be used for the Sun.

■ Use a combination of which ever style is best for the character. The Sun, for example, could be made with a hand-held torch behind crêpe paper or sweet cellophane decoration. Vayu and Indra could be body puppets with Vayu decorated in cotton wool clouds and Indra in silver and gold foil lightning flashes. Hanuman could be a jointed stick puppet.

You will also need to make a backdrop. The style of any backdrop used will vary with the type(s) of puppet. There is only one setting for this part of the story and this could be an Indian country scene or simply the sky.

Many children like the illusion of puppets moving with little or no visible support and this can be achieved by creating a theatre space, perhaps like a Punch and Judy show, which hides the operators whilst allowing the audience to see the puppets. The disadvantages of this approach are that it usually limits the style of puppets used and it creates a space in which only a small number of children can work as puppet operators.

A more open approach would be to set aside a large area of classroom wall for the backdrop against which any style of puppet can perform. Children soon become used to seeing the puppet operators and learn to focus on the action of the story.

Resource 14

ACTIVITY 3 Developing the dialogue

WHERE? In the classroom or hall.

HOW? Using puppets to develop and stimulate dialogue is a well-known technique. Although it is suggested here as a preparation for a performance of the Hanuman story using puppets, its value should not be seen as restricted to performances or formal presentations. In this case you may choose to use it to explore the story without ever developing this into something to share with others.

There are many ways of working with puppets and the following suggestions are not intended to be prescriptive or to represent a step-by-step process. As ever, take what seems useful and ignore the rest.

◆ *Tips for . . .* developing puppet dialogue

- Retell the story simply, and with pauses, to allow the children to use their puppets to enact or mime the story as you speak. Children can do this as individuals whilst sitting at their tables or in the story corner. You are aiming for a quiet, reflective time when children focus on listening to the story and moving their characters appropriately. You may well find that the quality of the children's listening is enhanced because they have things in their hands and permission to look at and move them while they hear the story, in much the same way that adults can become engrossed in a radio play or discussion whilst driving.

  It might be better to do this with very simple stick puppets (as on Resource Sheet 14) because these can be made relatively quickly and keep the more elaborate puppet construction until children are more familiar with the story.

- Discuss as a class the different types of voices that the characters will have. How will the god of the storm talk? What sort of voice will the god of the wind have? and so on.

- Use either simple puppets or those that the children have made in Activity 2, and allow the children to work in pairs to try out the story. Share out the parts so that each child has two characters. Allow the dialogue to develop naturally at this stage; it will probably consist of shared narration — questions about what happens next and some true dialogue.

- An alternative is to give pairs very small sections of the story such as: Hanuman plays with the Sun; Indra comes by and blows up a storm, etc.

- Develop the work on voices mentioned above, but this time in small groups, looking for exciting and diverse approaches, particularly to the voices of the gods. Children could try all speaking at once, or two speaking chorally and the others providing wind or storm effects (see Activity 4). They could experiment with talking into drums or tubes to create different effects.

- Encourage children to add their character's thoughts at key moments in the story. For example: 'I'm bored and it's so hot. There's nothing to play with, unless I play with the Sun . . . Why should I put the Sun down just because Indra says so? Oh no, he's going to zap me with a lightning bolt!'

- Children could be asked to go back over their scene or story and prepare it to show to the rest of the class. This will involve a process of rehearsal, shaping, choosing the best bits and getting them right. If you or a helper have time to work with the groups, and to provide an 'outside view', this will help tremendously to structure the children's work.

- Children could try working in groups of four, where two are the puppet operators and two provide the voices.

- For those who find the creation of dialogue really difficult, you could provide a tape of you telling the story to which the children have to add only the movement and sound effects. The tape could also have gaps in it for children to fill in specific parts of the dialogue as a first step.

- Allow children to make up their own parts of the story, which can be particularly useful if remembering the 'official' version is causing a block to the puppet work. This could include Hanuman playing before he gets bored, or a big celebration party at the end of the story. You could include extra characters such as Hanuman's friends and his mother, the monkey princess.

- Children could enact the scene where Hanuman tells his mother of the adventure once it is all over. This will be a good opportunity to practise the art of verbal narrative.

Activity 4 Organising a puppet play

WHERE? In the classroom or possibly the hall for performance.

HOW? The key organisational issue here is making sure that every class member can be involved and feel part of the story-telling.

Working in small groups to produce a number of different versions of the story can be effective. You will need to ensure that each group knows the story well enough to work in this way. Alternatively, ask different groups to tell only part of the story.

If you have the staff, split the class into two groups so that each group can work towards showing their puppet play to the other half of the class. This will work best if the groups are able to work on their plays at different times, so that they can have the performance space to themselves.

The various tasks in putting on a puppet play are:

■ **Puppet operators**   These need not be the same children throughout the whole performance, operators can swap around and different puppets of the same character can be used at different times. You could use this as an opportunity to make, for example, different versions of Vayu. A 'fast Vayu' for when he is seeking Hanuman, an 'angry Vayu' for the next scene and a 'happy Vayu' for the end of the story.

■ **Puppet voices**   Again these can be shared out and, because of the fantastic nature of the characters, some can speak chorally or with several voices at once. See the suggestions for developing dialogue in Activity 3 and the sound effect suggestions below.

■ **Sound effects**   This story is rich in opportunities for sound effects:

– The peaceful countryside or skyscape. Music could be used here and vocal sounds for birdsong and gentle wind. The swaying of branches and leaves in the wind could be created using rustling and waving paper.

– The bouncing Sun. Experiment with vocal sounds and drum sounds.

– Indra's elephant. Try vocal sounds through tubes of different lengths. Also heavy footfalls on a reverberating surface.

– Indra's storm. Vocal sounds, drums and percussion, peas in a round tin for rain.

– Indra's arrow. Vocal 'swishing sounds', also experiment with dragging objects across surfaces to try to get the right sound.

– Hanuman's fall to Earth. Descending glockenspiel or other percussion sounds. Descending ocarina or recorder notes?

– The storm dying and the air ceasing to move. A slowing down and quieting of the storm sounds above.

– The distress of every living thing. Vocal sounds based on a variety of animals. Leaves and trees shaking then becoming still.

– The air starting to move again. Reverse of the sounds above.

– The sounds of joy as life returns. Music, laughter, partying sounds, 'Hooray, bravo', etc.

■ **Music**   Music could accompany the story, mixing with the sound effects and opening and closing scenes.

Development across Key Stages 1 and 2 . . .

OTHER PUPPET PLAYS   Historical stories can be represented in a similar way. Pupils will need to research carefully to decorate and costume their puppet characters.

■ **Masks**   Children can act out the story of Hanuman using masks instead of puppets.

Parents and Grandparents

INTERVIEWS

Curriculum context

This provides ideas for an oral history project for Key Stage 2 – focused around the study unit 'Britain since 1930'. It could also be used as part of a local history project. It is targeted at Key Stage 2 but is easily adaptable for use in Key Stage 1 where the revised History National Curriculum requires that children should use 'adults talking about their own past' as part of their historical enquiry. In the use of the recording equipment there is a link to Technology.

Key Strategies

The two main Speaking and Listening strategies developed in these activities are the interview and the structured report on an historical enquiry.

Pupils will have the opportunity to question others in a formal interview – meeting with and listening to a range of speakers in the process. They will also have to consider the needs of their audience and the purpose of their communication as they organise and present their findings.

A range of possibilities for developing the work are also suggested including historical role-play.

Expected outcomes

■ teamwork

■ dealing confidently and sensitively with members of the public

■ balance of formal and informal use of language

■ finding language appropriate to the task.

How to use the material

This is necessarily presented as a set of open-ended suggestions since oral and local history will, by its very nature, be determined entirely by the local resources available to you.

We have provided a structure to help children develop their interview skills and to employ them towards a particular historical objective.

You will need

■ recording equipment.

ACTIVITY 1 Interviews in pairs

WHERE?   In the classroom in pairs.

HOW?   We are assuming that this is the beginning of the classwork on History study unit 'Britain since 1930'. The children will have placed 1930 on a class timeline and will be aware of how long a period is being studied and will have identified some aspects of the period.

The teacher will also have emphasised that their own history and the history of the adults around them is part of the history studied in this unit. So their aim now is to find out as much as possible about Britain since 1930 by interviewing people around them and recording their answers.

Children are used to talking to one another, asking and responding to questions, eliciting information, picking up inferences and generally quizzing one another. It's also the first instinct of a confident child, if an interesting visitor arrives in the class, to ask the visitor questions about himself/herself. Less confident children are usually no less curious about the visitor – all children need encouragement to frame and address their questions appropriately. In this activity we try to channel that natural curiosity into a formal interview.

First, try some games and simple activities which will focus the children on thinking about interviews.

CLOSED QUESTIONS   One partner chooses an object in the room and the other has to ask questions which will help them guess the object. The questions *must* be answerable by 'YES' or 'NO'. For example:

Question:	Is it on the walls?
Answer:	No.
Question:	Does it hang from the ceiling?
Answer:	No.
Question:	Is it on the floor?
Answer:	Yes.
Question:	Is it the carpet?
Answer:	No.
Question:	Does it have legs?
Answer:	Yes.
Question:	Is it a chair?
Answer:	Yes.

OPEN QUESTIONS   Again in pairs, the children take it in turns to ask each other questions about an aspect of their lives – 'How did you get to school this morning?' 'Do you have any hobbies?' etc.

The aim is to focus on open questions. No question should be answerable with 'YES' or 'NO'.

This can be given a more game-like feel if they work in groups of three with the third group member noting points against the interviewer every time a question is answered with 'YES' or 'NO'.

Illustrate what an open question is by examples:

Open questions:

■ What did you have for breakfast this morning?

■ How do you get to school?

■ What is your journey like?

Closed questions:

■ Did you have toast for breakfast?

■ Do you walk to school?

■ Is it a long way?

HISTORICAL QUESTIONS   Now ask the children to focus on a more historical set of questions, thinking about the interviewee's 'oldest living relative'. For example:

■ Who is your oldest living relative?

■ How old are they?

■ Where do they live?

■ What job do/did they do?

■ Were they alive during the Second World War?

■ Tell me anything particularly interesting that has happened to them.

You will clearly need to use a degree of sensitivity in introducing this exercise to ensure that children whose family life is perhaps more disrupted than that of others do not feel threatened by the questions.

With the focus being on the 'oldest living relative', however, there is a helpful distance between the child and the subject of the interview.

Ask the interviewer and the interviewee to note any questions to which they answered 'I don't know' as these will form fruitful areas for personal investigation in the history project – either as homework research or a possible focus for the interviews in Activities 2 and 3.

ACTIVITY 2 Interviewing a visitor SMALL GROUP TALK

WHERE? In small groups in the classroom, then in an interview space.

HOW? In this activity the children are going to practise their interview skills on a real but 'tame' adult. It could be a teacher or helper from another class, a parent or grandparent, the lollipop person or an assembly visitor.

You could use one visitor who is happy to be interviewed a number of times by different groups, or a range of visitors, one for each different group. Select someone whose life or work is of immediate interest to the pupils and who is old enough to be able to describe some notable changes in their own lifetime. A particularly fruitful possibility would be someone who also used to be at the school many years ago and can talk about changes in the school.

The emphasis in 'oral history' work is on interviewing individuals about their own lives – not on interviewing history professionals about changes that happened to other people.

You will need to decide in advance whether the interview is to be recorded. Recording it on tape or video may seem a daunting prospect but it will give children the chance to assess the quality of their own Speaking and Listening, as well as providing hard data for use in their own project work on the History unit.

◆ *Tips for . . .* oral interviews

It is vitally important to establish a focus for the interview. This focus will, however, be determined by who is chosen to be interviewed.

In the context of Britain since the 1930s the focus could be:

- the changes someone has seen in their working life

- someone's experiences of the Second World War: bombing, evacuation, rationing, etc

- how entertainment and leisure are different now from in previous decades.

Once the focus is established we suggest that you compile a list of questions to help the small groups to frame their interview. Then ask each small group to add questions to the list which cover the areas of particular interest to them.

- Begin with straightforward questions which set the interviewee and interviewer at ease.

- Ask questions which encourage the interviewee to express personal preferences – 'What do you most like/least like?'

- If you want pupils to investigate matters which are more personal to the visitor – e.g. the visitor's home life – do check out in advance that the interviewee is happy to be asked, and to answer, such questions.

- Do stress again that the pupils need to use open questions. Stress also that some subsidiary and clarifying questions will be necessary, and that they should not therefore be completely tied by their list of questions.

Ask the group to organise an interview space (or you could organise it for them). You will need comfortable chairs for the interviewer and their guest, a table for the tape recorder, a quiet location (especially if recording) which also puts the guest at their ease.

Within each small group there will need to be questioners, recorders, carers. Remember:

- Too many questioners can be off putting for the subject. On the other hand the questioners will find support in numbers.

- Recorders will need to be able to operate audio or video equipment and check recording quality without putting off the rest of the group.

- A carer needs to be able to look after the guest and their needs. This is not a soft option!

EXAMPLE Let's take the example of a retired woman who is an elderly relative of a child in the school and who is old enough to have experienced the Second World War as a child.

PREPARATION ■ The children have prepared a list of questions (examples overleaf).

■ They have allocated the questions in roughly equal numbers to different group members. To give structure to the interview these have been sorted under different headings.

■ They have made the practical arrangements – when and where the interview will take place. These factors may have been decided by the teacher, but it would be a valuable experience for the children to have to make some arrangements themselves or, at least, to telephone or write to confirm the details.

■ They have decided how they will record the responses. They will record the whole interview on a cassette. Since transcribing afterwards can be very slow and boring, some members of the group will also be making brief notes (on the question sheet), whilst the questioner concentrates on the subject and asks for any clarification. This kind of note-taking is quite an advanced skill (which is why having three scribes will be helpful).

LIST OF QUESTIONS

Ben

Questions about Mrs Andrew

How long have you lived in this area?

What do you like best about it?

What do you least like about it?

Satnam

Questions about the Second World War

How old were you during the Second World War?

Where did you live at that time?

What effect did the war have on your life?

Clare

Questions about Mrs Andrew's school days

Where did you go to school?

What was your favourite lesson?

What was your least favourite lesson?

How was school then different from school today?

Robert

Questions about Mrs Andrew's home

What was the kitchen like in the house where you lived when you were a child?

How is your kitchen today different?

What is the biggest change in people's kitchens which you have seen in your lifetime?

(We have used the kitchen examples because it is one of the rooms which has changed the most – but bathrooms and living rooms will also yield interesting comparisons)

CONDUCTING THE INTERVIEW

This is where children's Speaking and Listening skills are most in evidence.

The interviewers need to strike a balance between the formality and aim of the situation (it is not simply an interesting conversation, but has clear objectives and parameters), and the need to engage the subject in a conversational manner, thus 'getting the best out of' him or her.

Although this sounds daunting, many children instinctively grasp the correct register or tone of voice for given situations, though this is often masked by shyness or uncertainty.

ACTIVITY 3 Choosing who to interview

SMALL GROUP
PLANNING SESSION

WHERE?   In the classroom interview space (as in Activity 2) or on site.

HOW?   Depending on how wide a range of visitors you have used in Activity 2 this stage may not be necessary. The aim here is for pupils to identify another, contrasting adult, to interview and to plan and conduct the interview along the same lines as previously.

ACTIVITY 4 Reporting the interview(s)

GROUP WORK

WHERE?   In groups in class.

HOW?   The main consideration will be the purpose to which the research is to be put. For most purposes a written record of the interview is going to be much more useful than the taped version, and it is probably best to focus on the production of a written version of the interview.

■ It may be that the interview needs transcribing verbatim – in which case each group should type up one set of questions and answers on a word processor.

■ It may be that the class then wants to assemble a display from this database showing a range of answers to a given question about the period. In this case there should be a number of display panels relating to themes covered by the interviews: how work has changed; memories of the Second World War; how school has changed.

On each display panel pupils can write one or two relevant quotes from their interviewee(s) in a speech bubble. Make it clear through a drawing and a description who it is that said these things.

Other possible ways to report the interview are:

■ **As a newspaper report**   This needs to be lively, attention grabbing, full of information with an interesting headline and possibly an illustration.

■ **As a formal report**   Such as in an archive or as research which someone else can access and use – this should include copies of the question and, as far as possible, verbatim replies.

In some circumstances you may wish to ask children to make an oral presentation of their research. They could set it up as a talk to the whole class, covering: 'who we interviewed' (essential details about them); 'why we chose them'; 'what they said about . . . ' (choose two of their most interesting answers and play that excerpt from the tape).

Finally children may see the possibility within the information imparted by their interviewee to do their own dramatic reconstruction of an event: an incident during the blitz, for example, or an incident in a day at school. They could research costume and furnishings – asking their interviewee questions which might help to give a sense of period to their presentation.

Development across Key Stages 1 and 2...

Interviews with visitors or people outside the school community are an endlessly flexible way to help children acquire firsthand knowledge of the world *and* at the same time hone their Speaking and Listening skills. Here are just a few ways of using the potential of the interview in a range of curriculum contexts.

IN HISTORY   An oral history archive can be passed on from class to class or the whole school can be involved in contributing to it.

In other History study units the interview may still have a part to play: in studying the Tudors you could interview the education officer of a local museum which has Tudor artefacts; in studying Victorian Britain you could interview members of a local history society, etc.

IN GEOGRAPHY   There may be parents or children in the school who have travelled widely and may well have been born or lived in countries being studied in the Geography curriculum. They form a rich human resource for interviewing: and their recollections can impart a real sense of place of which textbooks or even videos may not be capable.

IN RE   Interviews with members of the various local faith communities can form the basis for much work through Key Stage 1 and Key Stage 2. If a similar template is applied to the questions addressed to each faith community, comparisons will be possible between the religions.

Recordings could also include samples of the music and singing distinctive to each religion.

The Forest People

DRAMA: TEACHER
IN ROLE

Curriculum context

This section provides a model for a whole class dramatic improvisation. The content of this model – the life of a self-contained community of forest people – makes it particularly relevant to the Geography curriculum (as this imagined world can both be based on geographic data previously introduced, or lead on to a class project looking at life in a distant locality). Depending on the direction in which you take the drama it can touch on a range of other curriculum areas.

Key Strategy

Drama can take many forms – there have already been a range of drama strategies presented in earlier sections. The aim of the drama activities in this section is for children to be able to build up a shared picture of another world, to improvise dialogue, to engage in role-play.

There are particular suggestions for the teacher to work in role. This can be a powerful drama strategy right across the curriculum, and a number of 'tips' are given as an aid to teachers who are new to this way of working.

The basic dramatic situation yields rich possibilities for developing a range of Speaking and Listening skills including story-telling, discussion, group decision making, formal and informal speech.

Expected outcomes

■ shared creativity in small and large groups

■ increased ability to talk in role

■ readiness to participate in group problem-solving.

How to use the material

There are a number of interlinked drama activities which are built around exploring a small, closed community of forest people.

The activities are probably best done in the order we have suggested.

The ideas presented here could certainly be sustained for two or three forty-minute drama sessions and could easily develop into more, perhaps lasting over a whole term.

ACTIVITY 1 Forest talk

WHERE?   In the drama space, with everyone together for discussion.

HOW?   In this first section, as you begin your drama, use discussion to build up a shared picture of what life might be like if you all lived in a forest. Build up the idea of a self-sufficient community whose needs are met from its environment – there is no 'outside'.

■ Agree a name for the forest people and for the forest.

■ Try to instil a sense of the independence of the forest people – of the balance of their lives. Try to dispel the notion that they are in any way backward because their lifestyle is not highly technological.

Allow the children to suggest the elements that make up a typical day, and also to suggest the necessary 'life support' activities if these are not forthcoming.

Write down the elements of the day on a large sheet of paper, perhaps using simple symbols for the different daily tasks. This may provide a good opportunity for working against children's stereotypes of gender roles.

Sun up	Wake up, wash in stream, gather fruit for breakfast.
Morning	Village meeting to choose task for the morning.
Rest of morning	Task – collecting fire-wood, cooking, hunting, house repairs.
Noon	Lunch – all together. Then sleep.
Afternoon	Village games.
Evening	Feast, tell stories, dance.
Night	Prayers, sleep.

ACTIVITY 2 **Creating the village**

WHERE?   In the drama space.

HOW?   Having established some idea of the forest people and how they live, you now move on to create the spaces in which the drama will happen.

An important consideration here is to decide how long you will want to sustain this first drama session and how often you will want to return to the 'forest' for future sessions.

Clearly the ideal would be to establish the different spaces and then leave them set up for future sessions, but this is unlikely to be possible. One option is simply to mark the various areas on the floor, but not to build extensive 'sets'. The marks can then be left or re-drawn each time. If you show their positions on a diagram, this can provide a useful map reading exercise.

If you can allow the children actually to construct the different areas, you can use a variety of materials:

■ PE benches and other equipment can be used to represent houses, caves, bushes and trees. These can be decorated with paper and card to extend the craft value of the exercise.

■ Use PE ropes and mats to mark off different areas for the meeting place, river, cooking area, etc.

You can also use the planning and building of the settlement to explore simple geographic ideas:

■ Why are the forest dwellers' homes near a river?

■ What will the houses be built from and how?

■ If they leave the village how will they travel?

■ Why are the houses close together?

■ If the forest people have to cross the river, how will they do so?

ACTIVITY 3 The forest dwellers' day

DRAMATIC IMPROVISATION

WHERE?   In the forest as built in Activity 2.

HOW?   This may well be the start of your next session if you have spent some time building the forest in the first session.

The idea is to give children an opportunity to explore their roles as forest people. Later on you will all develop a dramatic story together, but for now, simply allow time for the children to become used to the situation and to enjoy exploring their roles.

The simplest approach would be to begin at sunrise and work through your planned day as in Activity 1. You will be able to assist the process by becoming one of the forest people yourself at certain times (see 'Tips for teacher in role' on page 133), or speaking from outside the drama as appropriate. Use whichever approach gives the greatest clarity, organisation and control, and thus the maximum support for the children.

Sorting out jobs for the day would probably work best with you in role, helping to get things organised. You may feel, however, that you need to narrate a careful walk through the forest, and perhaps stop the drama and talk through the situation if you feel that some children are losing focus. This kind of teacher flexibility allows you to help the children to structure their dramatic play as well as helping to retain the sense of control and order that you are used to in other teaching situations.

◆ *Tips for . . .* teacher in role

- Adopting a role need not require any 'performance' or acting skills. Essentially, you will be speaking from someone else's point of view – slipping into their shoes and trying to see a dilemma or situation as they would. This allows the children to respond to the role, thus heightening the drama and their sense of involvement.

- Use the strategy flexibly. It cannot be overstressed that the teacher's input into any drama situation is vital and that fears of chaos and loss of control are no more relevant than in other areas of the curriculum. The teacher still has her full range of control and discipline strategies available. You can stay in role for as long or as short a time as necessary. You might spend just a few moments in role as a stimulus and then step out of role to facilitate discussion.

- Drama can be noisy, different groups of children can be spread out over a wide area, each actively engaged in pursuing their own part of the drama, and these factors do call for absolute clarity in organisation. Make sure that the children know what is expected of them in terms of behaviour and the limits of the situation (e.g. we remain in the hall), before you, and they, go into role.

- Have a clear signal which indicates to the children when you are in role and when you are speaking as yourself – the teacher. A simple hat, headband, scarf or perhaps an object that you carry in role can help here.

- Establish control strategies both within and outside the drama.

  - If I want to call the forest people together for a meeting I will go to the meeting place and blow three notes on my ocarina. That is a signal for you all to stop whatever you are doing and come at once to the meeting place to hear an important message.

  - If I want to stop our story about the forest people, I'll call you all over to sit around my chair. Make sure that you're ready to listen at once when I do that. Whenever I sit on my chair it means that the story will stop for a while.

- Either within or outside the drama, deal with episodes of inappropriate behaviour by calling everyone together. Examples of unfairness, silliness, etc. can be dealt with by calling a village meeting. This could sometimes lead to prevarication and justification which is better dealt with outside the drama.

If it is appropriate, you could end this section with a time when, as a class, you look back over the forest people's day and reflect upon it:

- How well did we work together as forest people?

- What was the most interesting part of the day?

- Who can tell the story of their day in the forest?

ACTIVITY 4 **Problems and opportunities**

WHERE?   In the 'forest' as in Activities 1 and 2.

HOW?   You can now use the situation of the forest people to explore a number of situations:

STRANGERS

You call a meeting and say that you have discovered footprints on the far side of the river, but they are not like those of your own people. Whose could they be?

Allow the children to discuss this. It might help to employ a simple control strategy here of using a 'speaking gourd'. This can be any object – a shell, stone, piece of bark, etc., which is passed to those who raise their hand to speak. They can only actually speak when they are holding the 'gourd'.

Allow the children to work through their ideas for what they should do. Perhaps some will want to fight the strangers, or defend the village. Others will have more friendly intentions. One interesting point here is to note the kind of vocal register that the children employ when speaking in the formal meeting situation. Do they respond to the need for a different kind of language to that which they will usually employ? Does the formality of the 'speaking gourd' assist this?

When you feel that the discussion has reached a suitable point, send everyone off to work as usual but with a suggestion that they think over all that has been said as they work.

How can the drama develop from here?

■ You could find a gift from the strangers (a piece of art work, perhaps a shovel or other tool). Call a meeting and decide how to respond. Should you all leave a gift in the same place and what should it be?

■ You could use narration, to settle everyone to sleep. In the night they hear rustlings and other strange sounds. The next morning, they talk about what the sounds could be and perhaps set up a watch the following night, each ready with a greeting, or a warning for the strangers. You could break the class drama at this point, to allow the children to work out still pictures of the first meeting between the forest people and the strangers.

■ You could go into role as one of the strangers, asking the forest people for their help. Perhaps your settlement down river has been flooded, or you've heard of their way of life and want to come to live with them.

DANGERS

Introduce, again at a meeting, the idea that there is some danger threatening the community. Perhaps the river is rising, or the fish are dying, maybe a volcano is threatening to erupt.

The responses to these dangers can be various, from physical activity like building a dam, to some villagers leaving the settlement to seek out the cause of the pollution that is killing the fish. In this scenario, you could return as someone from 'outside' whom the villagers must convince to change their ways.

In terms of drama, these options can be explored through continuing the story as before, or through the use of still pictures, mime or sound pictures. There is also the possibility of creating ritualised movements and sounds as the children work together to build the dam, or perform a dance to appease the fiery mountain.

FESTIVAL

Prepare for and enact a festival to celebrate the life of the forest people. The festival could include singing and dancing, story-telling, poems, art and craft. It could procede around the whole village with appropriate activities at the river, the cooking area, around the houses and at the meeting place. There are clear links with RE here and the work could well spread out of the drama into other classroom activities.

CENSUS

The forest people decide to map and measure their village, count their animals, write down the names of all the people and where they live. This activity, useful in itself and linking with Maths and Geography, could be used as the starting point for a further drama situation. Perhaps you reveal that since the last census a valuable statue has been destroyed. What should replace it? Ideas, which demonstrate the values of the forest people, could be drawn, modelled, or made in still pictures (which can also be moved and 'modelled').

Another possible scenario is that as a result of the census the forest people decide that they are growing too numerous and will have to split, forming a colony. But who will go, how and where to?

Development across Key Stages 1 and 2...

IN GEOGRAPHY The geographic potential of this dramatic activity can be developed by emphasising the contrasts between this group and the life of communities in other localities.

Geographic phenomena such as natural hazards can be introduced as a factor into the drama.

IN ENGLISH Pupils can develop an alternative language for their community. This could be built up over time; to start with they simply give new names to objects, and eventually they try to have conversations in their new language. They could use the rules of English, or they could create new ones. This is an effective way of reflecting on the rules of English.

They could consider whether one form of address is particularly appropriate for addressing the leader of the forest people and another for the ordinary villagers.

IN SCIENCE Many aspects of the Science curriculum can be touched upon in these activities.

Some of the basic classifying skills of the Science curriculum can be introduced into the drama: classification of living things within the village, into edible, inedible, etc.

The importance of basic life processes can also be illustrated vividly – what happens if the food or water supply runs out or is infected for example? What if strangers bring new diseases or harmful substances into the village? A plant which is an important source of food is mysteriously dying – what do the children think (within the drama) could be responsible? What do plants need? What is missing in the village? etc.

STRATEGIES AND ACTIVITIES FOR Y5/Y6

Saying 'No'

Curriculum context

Teachers are all too aware of the need to help children avoid and rebuff unwelcome interference from adults or older children – and at various stages through Key Stage 1 and Key Stage 2 the subject will probably need to be tackled head on in school, perhaps within the PSHE context.

We suggest here an approach to this aspect of children's personal and social education using the drama strategy of Forum Theatre. The aim is to help pupils develop and to trust their own judgement in difficult situations they might face.

Key Strategy

Forum Theatre is a flexible, adaptable educational drama strategy. By focusing on particular issues within a structured, large group discussion the whole class can participate in the drama, sharing their ideas, insights and opinions, making relevant contributions, recognising the worth of opposing ideas, and developing a sense of the complexity of a given situation. Forum Theatre is mediated by the teacher and operates within a clear, simple framework, minimising the danger of loss of control or dissipated focus.

Expected outcomes

■ increased confidence in dealing with difficult situations

■ enhanced ability in drama

■ improved ability to focus attention during group discussion.

How to use the material

In this section we provide:

■ an introduction to Forum Theatre and its usefulness

■ a worked example of Forum Theatre in action

■ some tips for using Forum Theatre

■ four suggested scenarios for using Forum Theatre.

WHERE?

In the hall or in a cleared classroom space.

About Forum Theatre

It can be extremely difficult to equip children to cope with unwelcome interference from adults or older children, particularly that which leads to emotional, physical or sexual abuse. We can give children rules of behaviour – for example the well-known 'Stranger Danger' rules. These are an important starting point. They have their limitations, however, not least in the difficulty of defining 'stranger'. Your new Head Teacher is a stranger, as is the woman with children who asks directions to the park. Add to this the fact that most abuse is perpetrated by adults known to the children concerned, and it is clear that simple slogans and messages, while they may have their place, are not enough.

It is equally important for pupils to develop their own sense of judgement. Drama, and Forum Theatre in particular, is an ideal medium through which to achieve this deepening of judgement, as the whole class examine a dilemma together and are encouraged, collectively, to make judgements about the situation and to suggest possible solutions.

The situations or dilemmas we suggest are not all, by any means, 'heavy' or highly charged, but they do all deal with the kind of choices that children have to make as they develop their independence and know their own mind – essential qualities in growing up.

The strength of Forum Theatre is that it provides an opportunity to discuss the possible outcomes of actions and words and, through drama, explore these possible outcomes. The whole process is designed to give children greater confidence in saying 'No', and in extracting themselves from situations which they sense could be dangerous.

This is not a formula for solving those desperate, though thankfully rare, occasions when children are at risk from adults, but it should be seen as part of their continuing Personal, Social and Health Education.

In essence, Forum Theatre involves:

Stage 1. Defining an area in which the enactment will take place.

The simplest, and probably best, approach is to have the class sitting in a circle and agreeing that the centre of the circle is where the drama happens.

Stage 2. Introducing a clear scenario to begin the drama.

This may grow naturally out of your current work and be suggested by children or the teacher.

In many cases, the teacher will set up the scenario at the beginning of the session, choosing something which opens up a particular issue:

■ Two children find a five pound note on the way to school. What should they do with it?

■ During the Second World War, a family must decide whether to evacuate the children.

■ Three children are struggling home from school, carrying a large woodwork project. A man stops and offers a lift.

Stage 3. Choosing initial 'actors' to enact the starting point whilst everyone else watches.

Stage 4. Stop at appropriate points and accept children's suggestions. Make collective decisions about re-running the scene with different outcomes, introducing new elements, swapping 'actors', etc. This is the key to Forum Theatre, the sense that things can be tried again, changed around, we can see 'what happens if . . . '

You must choose the point at which to move on, to develop the scenario, or to leave it, perhaps exploring it further through discussion, personal writing, art etc.

It is also important to understand the centrality of discussion, of involving everyone in what is happening and exploring the nuances and implications of the events in the drama. This is the core skill of handling Forum Theatre and we can probably best explore this by a detailed example:

FOR EXAMPLE: THE FIVE POUND NOTE

You want your class to explore concepts of honesty and ownership.

You are using Forum Theatre. You set up a scenario in which two children find a five pound note on the way to school.

Having settled the class in the space (Stage 1) and explained the scenario (Stage 2), you choose two children to enact the moment of finding the money (Stage 3).

This is how you might proceed through Stage 4:

Teacher	Class
	James and Lubna are shy at first, wary of everyone watching them. They stand around and look embarrassed.
You ask the class for ideas as to how they can actually show this important moment. Someone suggests that they should walk along and Lubna should stop James because she's seen something sticking out of the hedge.	
	James and Lubna try this out, but again they stop, after Lubna points at the money.
You ask the class for suggestions as to what they should say and a simple dialogue emerges.	
	James and Lubna start to say what has been suggested and then begin to add more words of their own.
	LUBNA Look, what's that? JAMES It's money. LUBNA Five pounds. JAMES What should we do with it? LUBNA Take it to Mrs Marshall. JAMES Yeah.
Now ask the class for their views on what these two children have just done. Point out that it is possible for children to react differently and ask for volunteers to show what could have happened. To distance the actions in the drama from the 'actors' playing the roles, it might be a good idea to give the roles fictional names at this point.	
	Two more children re-play the scenario and this time an argument develops. One wants to give the money to the school, the other wants to keep it.
It looks like the one who wants to keep the money is running out of arguments, so you ask the class to suggest what she might say. Someone suggests that she wants the money to buy her sister a birthday present, so you feed this in.	

At this point you 'freeze' the drama and ask those watching to speak the thoughts of the two characters involved. A picture of uncertainty emerges, each child (role) is unsure of the actions they have taken.

The argument continues, but in the end they decide to split the money 50/50.

Asking the two children to rejoin the circle, you pause at this point to discuss the story so far and any similar experiences of 'conscience' situations that the children have had.

This scenario could be developed in a number of ways:

■ We see what happens when one child goes home and her mum discovers the money.

◆ *Tips for . . .* **using Forum Theatre**

If you are new to Forum Theatre, then both class and teacher will need practice and reassurance as they develop their skills in this type of drama. The best advice is to try something out and keep persevering as everyone gets used to the strategies needed to make it work. It really is worthwhile in the long run as this type of drama can be a very powerful tool for exploring issues and situations.

■ Get the class used to the idea that when they enact a role, they are not being themselves, so it's perfectly admissible for a boy to step into a girl's role and vice versa. This freedom also allows children to readily adopt roles of older (or younger!) people, authority figures or any role which is different from their own background and experience.

■ Forum Theatre works best when focused on an issue or dilemma, so try to avoid giving a sense of there being a 'right' answer which the drama is merely seeking to illustrate. If children feel that, within the drama, they cannot explore a certain course of action, or make a particular statement, because 'Miss won't like it', then the drama will be diminished, less 'real' and hamper the children's ability to explore their dilemma truly from the inside.

■ This is not to suggest, however, that the normal rules of behaviour or conduct are suspended. The drama takes place within a specified physical area so, for example, an act of vandalism can be enacted without the danger of real vandalism.

■ Controlled and focused strategies can be utilised for violent scenes (see Activity 1 'Bully').

■ The kind of language which is acceptable will vary from teacher to teacher and from school to school. If something is said which is deemed inappropriate in a school setting (and which causes giggling or other loss of focus) this is a clear case for stopping the drama in order to re-establish what is acceptable and how the drama can proceed with alternative words or phrases.

■ However you use it, and whatever the theme of the drama, Forum Theatre should involve everyone.

■ It is important to keep asking the 'audience' for suggestions, to swap roles and introduce new elements frequently and to pause every so often so that the issues raised can be discussed.

■ As in all drama, children will develop their skills as they go along, but it's important to stress that the ability to 'perform' in front of others is not essential in this type of drama. Its strengths lie in its focus on issues and situations and the fact that everyone can participate.

■ One child decides, in the end, to tell his teacher. What does the other child do?

■ At the school assembly, an appeal is put out for five pounds, lost from someone's bag on the way to school. The money had been collected for charity.

In the following activities we give a number of starting points for using Forum Theatre to explore issues of trust and judgement.

ACTIVITY 1 Bully FORUM THEATRE EXAMPLE

One child has some sweets and other, bigger children gang up on him. The child tries to say 'No', but the sweets are taken anyway and he is left with a warning not to tell any teachers. What should he do?

This scenario starts with a physically threatening situation, and these are prone to difficulties and loss of focus. You could:

■ Start after the event – placing someone in the middle of the circle to be the bullied boy, while everyone else offers advice on what he should do.

■ Start as above, but let the first activity be one where the rest of the group speak the thoughts of the bullied boy.

■ Ask the participants to enact the bullying and taking of the sweets in three 'frozen' still pictures. Again, the rest of the group can speak thoughts as each picture is formed.

This scenario could be developed in a number of ways, including scenes with friends, family and teachers.

The important points are to encourage the class to find positive strategies to deal with bullying and to allow discussion of the children's own experiences. You can use the distance of role (the fact that we are all pretending these things are happening to someone else), to allow children to explore their own experiences and feelings in a less threatening manner.

ACTIVITY 2 School fair

At the school fair, some children are running a stall selling second-hand toys and books. One child has given a game in good condition and wants to sell it for £1.

An adult (or teenager) is hunting for bargains, and offers 50p for the game, which the child refuses. The adult repeatedly comes back and, as the afternoon goes on, becomes more insistent that the game be sold cheaply.

This simple scenario offers an opportunity for children to stick to their position and reject persuasive arguments, but in a highly structured and generally safe environment. The situation could develop in the following ways:

■ The adult returns with others so that the persuasion becomes bullying.

■ A teacher comes round and says that with only half an hour left, all prices should be reduced, but the child still feels that the game is worth more.

■ The child decides to withdraw the game from the sale and take it home again, but can she do this or should she be required to buy back the game because she's given it to the school to sell?

ACTIVITY 3 New teacher

A group of children are walking home from school when a car pulls up. The man inside says he's a new teacher going to start at the school next term. He wants a look around, and wonders whether anyone has time to show him the school. He'll give a lift home afterwards.

The key point here, of course, is that, as the children don't know the man, they shouldn't accept a lift with him, but it's given added tension by the fact that the man claims to be a teacher – an authority figure.

In your explorations of this scenario, the obvious end point is that the children all say a firm 'No' and the man drives off. This makes a point and could be the start of a discussion but there are further possibilities. You will clearly want to avoid any scene in which the man in the car uses force, keeping the focus on the children and their actions.

Other developments could be:

■ The Head Teacher arrives on the scene and wants to know who the children are talking to. Does she recognise the man in the car? If she does, and he is a new teacher, what will she think of his actions? We could see a scene in the Head Teacher's office as she talks to the new teacher.

■ Next term the new teacher and the same group of children meet in school – what do they say to each other? Does the teacher apologise for his actions?

ACTIVITY 4 Fireworks

Some children are in a newsagent's shop looking at fireworks. The shopkeeper notices their interest and says that, as they look like sensible children, he's prepared to bend the law and sell them some, as long as they don't tell anyone.

The conflict here rests on the fact that the children know that they are under age and shouldn't buy the fireworks, but that a persuasive adult is offering to break the law, 'no questions asked'.

The drama will clearly be enhanced if the children are tempted by the offer, so you may need to feed this into the scenario.

Other developments could be:

■ The children are caught by someone as they come out of the shop with the fireworks – a Police Officer, parent, teacher.

■ The children must decide whether to report the shopkeeper.

■ The purchase of the fireworks is followed by a number of consequences (perhaps discussed and then enacted or explored in still pictures and/or speaking thoughts):

- a firework accident

- the children being called to the Head Teacher

- the children are asked to say where they bought the fireworks.

13

Fear

Curriculum context

This unit includes a range of activities linked to PSHE curriculum objectives.

Key Strategies

In this section we use a number of strategies: radio adverts, class discussion and a performance poem to help pupils voice, discuss and confront fears.

Expected outcomes

■ enhanced vocabulary

■ imaginative use of language

■ enthusiasm for further work to explore the theme

■ vocal input from all members of the class.

How to use the material

The ideas here attempt to give children both space and structure to talk about fear – an important aspect of their emotional lives.

The five activities are independent of each other, exploring the theme in different ways. Any section would work on its own or with others.

Activities 4 and 5 are more 'personal' and potentially a more threatening approach to the subject than Activities 1–3. They might be inappropriate in classes where there is not an atmosphere of trust. They are certainly not initial activities to be attempted 'cold', but could be built upon what has gone before.

You will need

■ a prepared list of categories of fear (see page 148).

ACTIVITY 1 'Don't miss it!'

WHERE? In groups around tables or desks.

HOW? Ask groups to come up with a radio advertisement for a new, frightening film.

It might help to break the task up into the following sections:

1. Make up a title for the film and have some idea of the story.

2. List appropriate and atmospheric words that convey the mood of the film and give a sense of its scary nature.

3. Write the text of the advert.

4. Give out the parts and find a way of indicating who does/says what. Marker pens would be useful here.

5. Rehearse.

After some working time, listen to the results from each group. This activity should provide plenty of fun and it doesn't matter if some children take this less than seriously. Indeed, you could make the point that what is frightening to one person seems foolish to another, and that what frightened us as young children is different to what frightens us later in life.

ACTIVITY 2 Categories of fear

WHERE? This is a whole class discussion so it should happen in whatever space you and your class feel most comfortable in. Note that the outcomes will need to be recorded and this may affect how the space is used.

HOW? Ask the question, 'What types of fear are there?'

As an aid and stimulus to the discussion have some headings prepared under which fears can be listed:

■ **Safety fears** Things which we are frightened of or respectful of for our safety.

■ **Imaginary fears** Frightening things which we imagine.

■ **Irrational fears** Things which we know cannot harm us but which we still fear.

'Irrational fears' will need some explanation – you may prefer a substitute such as 'Foolish fears'.

You might select other categories, or these may arise and be added during the discussion.

You could simply make the list on a blackboard, or give large sheets of paper and marker pens to individual children who each collect one category of fear.

Use the categories and lists as a focus for the discussion, but be prepared to allow the talk to flow and develop. The structure should help to facilitate discussion on what could otherwise be too personal a subject. You might feel it appropriate to ensure that you end on an upbeat note, perhaps stressing the usefulness of fear – a little bit of fear before a performance can give an 'edge'. Sometimes fear helps you to avoid danger.

ACTIVITY 3 'I'm not scared . . . ' SMALL GROUP PERFORMANCE POEM

WHERE? In groups with some space to work, either around desks or tables or in a large space such as a hall.

HOW? Give out copies of the poem on Resource Sheet 15, page 150.

Ask the children to work in groups to perform the poem, thinking about:

- Who will say which lines?

- Which lines will work best said by everyone?

- How will you get the best out of the end of the poem?

The poem repeats one line many times to help those who have difficulty with reading.

You might find it helpful to go through the poem all together first and to give some examples of rhythm, pace and projection – depending on the experience and ability of your class in this kind of work.

End this part of the session by hearing the performances, then initiate a whole class discussion looking at the following questions:

- What do you think of the person in the poem?

- Is he or she brave or foolish?

- Is the person in the poem telling the truth?

- What answers might he or she give to the question at the end?

I'm not scared

I'm not scared of nothing, me
Not scared of my brother
Not scared of my mum
Not scared by the big kids
Scared of – no one
I'm not scared of nothing, me.

I'm not scared of nothing, me
Not scared of tomorrow
Not scared of today
Not scared of teachers
Not scared, no way
I'm not scared of nothing, me.

I'm not scared of nothing, me
Not scared, give me any dare
Not scared to dodge a car
Not scared to nick a car
Not scared of no police car
I'm not scared of nothing, me.
I'm not scared of nothing, me.

Alright then, I dare you to turn down your next dare.
Or are you scared?

ACTIVITY 4 'I was frightened when . . . '

WHERE? In any space where children can sit in a circle.

HOW? This is a simple exercise where, sitting in a circle, children take it in turns to complete the sentence, 'I was frightened when . . . '

This works best if you require the whole class to participate. It need not touch on children's secret fears or personal lives since the question can always be answered with reference to the past: 'I was frightened when I was five and I thought I'd drown in the sea.'

The usefulness of the exercise is the range of types of fear that children can refer to:

- 'I was frightened when I first came to this school.'

- 'I was frightened watching a film last night.'

- 'I was frightened of aeroplanes until I went on one.'

- 'I was frightened of the dark when I was little.'

NB: There is always the possibility that an exercise like this will reveal something particularly worrying, for example, 'I'm frightened of going to my Uncle's . . . '

If such a fear is voiced it would clearly need to be dealt with in an appropriate way – outside the context of this exercise. The danger of revealing deep and real concerns should, however, never prevent us from giving children space and structure for talking about their emotional lives.

ACTIVITY 5 'Mr Gibson's fear'

WHERE?   If 'Teacher in role' is used, then in the same space as, and continuing on from, the previous exercise back in the classroom.

HOW?   Mr Gibson is an imaginary person who is frightened of moving to a new town. He feels that no-one will want to know him, that he won't 'fit in'.

The character is used as a focus for exploring some of the concerns above, so his particular fear could easily be adapted to fit the concerns of your class.

You can represent Mr Gibson in a number of ways:

■ You could adopt the role of Mr Gibson and use 'Teacher in role' (see page 133) as the focus of the discussion.

■ You could produce a letter from him expressing his fears and discuss what the class may put in their response.

■ You could use a photograph as an initial stimulus and then ask the class what they would say to him to help overcome his fear. To deepen the discussion, be prepared to answer with the kind of things which Mr Gibson might say in response.

■ After a general discussion, you could ask the children to write letters to Mr Gibson and then have a selection read out.

Remember that the central focus of the activity is purposeful structured talk, in this case helpful suggestions which will make Mr Gibson less afraid.

UNIT 14

Ecology

Curriculum context

Many children are concerned about issues of ecology – the destruction of environment and habitat, the extinction of species, and a host of related issues from recycling to the testing of products on animals or the transportation of live animals. In this section we present strategies for exploring these issues, digging deeper into the arguments on both sides of the debate.

Key Strategies

The 'class debate' can be a powerful tool for developing children's Speaking and Listening skills. In this section therefore we outline six possible strategies for a class debate which will:

■ encourage children to voice their own ideas, insights and opinions with increased confidence

■ encourage them to present their ideas clearly, and fit their communication to the needs of an audience

■ allow children to listen to a range of speakers, and to consider and respond to an argument.

Expected outcomes

■ confidence in public speaking

■ lively debate

■ practice in shaping and delivering coherent arguments

■ assessment opportunities relating to quality of communication, quality of information and quality of argument.

How to use the material

Many classroom discussions can either fail to get started or be too one-sided. More formal structures for discussion and debate can help overcome this. They can help pupils to think through the issues, examine arguments and to arrive at a consensus, a majority view or, perhaps more often, to recognise that a variety of different attitudes exist.

All class discussions are to some extent formalised. Putting up hands when you wish to speak, waiting until the teacher asks for comments, listening when asked to, are all examples of the way that discussions are structured. The strategies in this section simply take this further.

In our experience the best debates are those where proponents and audience have undertaken some research into the subject. The debate is more informed and the arguments more persuasive. We therefore envisage that this debate follows on from work on an ecology-related topic.

There is also scope for using debate as an 'initiator', in that it will throw up issues that call for further exploration.

You will need

■ a prop (such as the speaking gourd).

ACTIVITY 1 An ecology debate

WHERE?   Location will depend on which of the suggested strategies you adopt.

HOW?   1.   Choose a strategy or structure for your debate.

2.   Identify an interesting and controversial viewpoint for the debate.

DEBATE STRATEGIES   ■ **Speaking gourd**   As a way of controlling a discussion to which many children wish to contribute, you can use the device of a 'speaking gourd' which can be any object which may be passed around the circle and which permits the holder to speak. No-one may speak unless they have the 'gourd'.

Those who wish to speak can raise their hand and when the present speaker has had their say, they can pass the 'gourd' around the circle until it arrives at the next person with a raised hand.

If many people have their hands raised, this can become unfair because of the possibility of individuals missing their turn when the gourd goes to someone who has only just put up their hand.

An alternative here is for the speaker, when finished, to get up and take the gourd to the next person, who may be indicated by the teacher. The gourd can also be simply passed around the circle continuously, giving each child the chance to speak or to pass the gourd on.

For the use of this technique in a drama context, see 'The Forest People' (page 129).

■ **Hot seating**   A person who has a particular view takes the hot seat. They can then be questioned by anyone and asked anything of relevance to the debate.

Those listening take careful note of what is said so that they can come back to the person in the hot seat if they detect inconsistencies.

■ **Balloon debate**   The classic balloon debate can be a powerful vehicle for the examination of issues and ideas as well as personalities. Children will need to identify an individual who represents their views on this subject – someone who not only has an opinion but has a plan of action about it.

The person could be fictitious or real. There is nothing to stop a speaker inventing an animal rights campaigner who intends to block a lorry load of sheep as it boards a ship.

Each speaker is allowed to make a brief statement about themselves and their plan of action and is then questioned on their views by the rest of the class.

The activity ends with a vote on who should be kept and who ejected!

■ **Formal debate**   In the classic formal debate a motion is proposed. There is a first and second on each side. Members of the audience ask questions and then vote on the motion at the end.

In school situations it may be better to have small teams proposing and opposing a motion, since this gives more support and also allows for a team investigation into the issues before the debate.

It also permits, if you split the class into six groups, for two groups to be involved in presenting any one debate whilst the remaining four groups are the 'audience', who get their turn to present the debate (on a different topic) in due course.

■ **Market of ideas**   The class is split between those who want to argue a particular point of view (the market traders), and those who will vote (the customers).

The market traders work in teams of two or three, each team representing a different point of view. For example, one team may argue that animal experiments should be allowed for medical research, another team may argue that animals should not be used in this way, whilst a third believes that animal testing should be allowed for deadly diseases.

Each team sets up its stall – a space in the market, perhaps marked by a table or row of chairs. The teams may not come out from behind their stalls.

As the customers enter the market they go round from stall to stall, listening to the arguments and arguing with the traders. Each customer has one token which they can spend at which ever stall convinces them of the value of their argument.

After a while a halt is called and the stall which has the most tokens has won the debate!

■ **Delegates**   The class is split into two roughly equal teams, according to their views on a particular issue.

Each team runs through the arguments in favour of their point of view and chooses someone to argue their case.

The teams sit opposite each other and the two delegates move into the space in the middle and begin to argue the issue.

Each team has a bat and when they hold it up the delegate must return to the team who then give further suggestions as to what to say.

They can also swap delegates, giving someone else from the team a chance to represent their views.

If a team member becomes convinced by the opposing team's arguments they can swap sides.

STATEMENTS FOR DEBATE   People are more important than animals and plants, so it does not matter if natural habitats are destroyed to make room for people and their crops.

Fancy printed packaging should be banned. It costs money and causes pollution. Things should only be sold in plain wrappers made from recycled paper and card.

This school should only buy recycled paper and books made from recycled materials.

Everyone should be required to eat a healthy diet with lots of fruit and vegetables.

All animal hunting should be banned.

No animal should be killed for food.

It is wrong to kill any animal, even an insect.

Cars should be banned because of the pollution they cause. People should be forced to use bicycles or public transport instead.

People should be made to pay for the roads they use.

Dropping litter should carry a heavy fine.

Dumping rubbish in the countryside should be punishable with prison.

Rubbish should be dumped in space.

Anyone who makes a noise after 10.00 pm at night and before 8.00 am in the morning should be fined.

There should be a tax on sweets and ice-creams to pay for extra street cleaners.

Every home should have different litter bins for paper, glass, plastic and other rubbish so that they can be recycled.

Zoos should be given money by the government.

Zoos should be banned and all the animals returned to the wild.

◆ *Tips for . . .* **running a class debate**

Encourage pupils to see that the debate involves everyone. Even when you are not speaking, you should be listening. Listening is an active process – it involves hearing, considering and responding.

Encourage pupils to be focused in their listening by asking such questions as:

- Does this argument make sense?
- Does this tie in with what the speaker has said before?
- Do I believe this is true?
- Do I believe this is fair?
- Is this relevant to the debate?
- Do I need anything to be made clearer?
- Do I need extra information?
- How does this person know this information or fact?

In their response children can:

- request clarification
- challenge the facts used by the speaker
- challenge the opinions of the speaker
- agree with the speaker and add supporting arguments of their own.

In all contributions encourage pupils to:

- make one point only
- make that point as clearly as they can
- be ready to back up their argument with facts as well as opinions.

Most importantly pupils should be encouraged to see the need to make their contribution relevant to what has gone before.

Evacuees

Curriculum context

This drama activity could form part of a class History project or topic on the Second World War, particularly on 'evacuation' and 'The Home Front'.

Key Strategies

This section uses a range of drama strategies including role-play and improvisation – leading to small group play making.

Pupils have the opportunity to evaluate their own and others' contribution to the drama.

Expected outcomes

■ greater understanding of, and empathy with, the situation of evacuees

■ enthusiasm for further work exploring the theme

■ greater confidence in using drama to explore issues and themes.

How to use the material

We offer four related drama approaches to exploring the theme of evacuees.

These could be used consecutively or independently within continuing topic work as appropriate.

The ideas vary in complexity from simple still pictures to more complex small group plays.

The ideas could also be linked to prose (letter writing 'in role', for example) and poetry, which could then be used to add depth to the drama.

Another important and valuable link would be with published fiction such as *Carrie's War* or *Tom's Midnight Garden*.

Useful material can be found in 'Tips for Teacher in Role' in the forest people unit (page 133), and the section on Forum Theatre in the Saying 'No' unit (page 142).

You will need

■ labels for Activity 3.

Activity 1 Go, don't go

WHERE? In a drama space, with enough room for group work.

HOW? This section is designed to build on curriculum work about evacuees. It will work best if children know about the situation, the reason for the proposed evacuation and the kinds of tensions and issues that this would raise.

Split the class into family groups, and give each 'family' a working space.

The children can choose their roles within the family. Not all the families need to have the same make up. It may be that the father is in the army, or he may be at home; there may be grandparents living at home. Whatever combination the children choose, encourage them to have at least two children in the family who are facing possible evacuation.

The drama starts when one of the adults explains that they have to make a decision about whether to evacuate the children because of the bombing. The options are:

- for the children to stay at home

- for the children to evacuate with their mother

- for the children to evacuate on their own.

You could also build in other factors such as a stiff and starchy relative who lives in the country, but a long way away. Would it be better to send the children to her, or for them to take their chances with an unknown host family closer to home?

◆ Tips for . . . role work

- Ensure that everyone is clear about the task and the necessary background information. Stress that the drama will begin when you say so, and that the children will then step into the shoes of the family grappling with this issue. They are not to plan the conversation or prepare a scene to show to others, they are simply to enact it as if it is happening now.

- If your class are new to this way of working, be prepared to help individual groups to re-focus. It's not uncommon for the possibilities of the situation to exceed your brief, and for children to find their houses bombed while they talk, or to be street fighting with an invading army. Part of the learning process, both in terms of drama skills and in relation to the topic, can be to stop the drama and discuss together why certain attitudes or actions are inappropriate.

- You might choose to share aspects of the drama with the whole class. Try to avoid this being seen as a performance, but more as an opportunity to look into each house and see what is going on. Ask everyone to stop for a moment whilst you all watch one particular house as they continue their discussion, then stop that household and ask another to pick up their own conversation for a few moments, and so on.

- At the end of this section of the drama, call everyone together and hear the decisions (if any) reached in each household and the reasons for them.

ACTIVITY 2 **Dreamtime**

WHERE?   In the drama space as in Activity 1.

HOW?   There will be powerful emotions attached to the story, and the device of a dream can be used to explore these without putting children 'on the spot'.

As so often in drama, the fiction and the strategies used can offer a safe 'distance' enabling children to explore and deal with complex and emotive themes.

Explain that it is the night after the discussion of the possibility of evacuating the children. Everyone is going to sleep.

The use of space is important here. Keep to the family groupings, but with everyone spread out a little, so that each person has their own space in which to lie on the floor.

If children are too close during this type of exercise, the 'embarrassment factor' can take over, and the temptation to nudge someone becomes irresistible!

Use narration to settle everyone:

> The house is quiet, you think everyone's asleep, but you can't get the conversation out of your mind. Think back over what was said.

> Are you worried as you try to get to sleep? Worried about being sent away from home? Or, if you're a parent, do you wish that you didn't have to send your children away, or are you concerned about their safety because of the bombing?

> What are you thinking and feeling as you lie there in the quiet house? What's going to happen to you?

> At long last you fall asleep, but the thoughts are still going round in your head, they won't go away, and you dream a dream.

> Think through your own dream as you lie there, what pictures will you see in your mind, what voices and sounds will you hear?

It might be a good idea to play some music at this point to help the children to focus on their dream. Something that is not too specific, but simply adds a sense of atmosphere. Something amorphous and not too rhythmic would be ideal. It need only last a minute or so.

Call the class back in to sit in a circle to describe their dreams.

Ask the children to pick out some of the common images from the dreams – perhaps being abandoned, losing luggage or possessions, being bombed?

Ask children, one by one, to move into the centre of the circle and form a still picture of one moment in their own dream. Gradually a picture is formed as each individual adds his or her 'statue' to the whole. Encourage them to relate to other people in the picture if they can so that the picture builds as a whole rather than in individual units.

You could then replay the dream music and ask the children to move, just for a few seconds before freezing again. Encourage slow, dreamlike movements.

You could also add some of the voices and phrases from the earlier family discussions, either spoken by you or some of the children, for example, repeated phrases such as 'You're going . . . ', 'Leaving home . . . ', 'Evacuate, evacuate', and so on.

Back in a circle again discuss the elements that might be used to create a dream drama:

- repeated phrases

- slow motion movements

- simple actions or words happening again and again

- a central point around which everything else happens

- a loss of the logic of everyday actions.

Ask each small 'family group' to choose elements from the family discussions and their own individual dreams, and build these into a group dream. Stress the need for something short and focused on one aspect of the dreamer's worries or fears.

ACTIVITY 3 **The village hall**

WHERE?   In the drama space, as before, or possibly in a real village hall!

HOW?   The 'cattle auction' where lonely and uncertain children meet their host families for the first time is one of the strongest images of evacuation.

The idea of this activity is to give some sense of what that experience might have been like. You could turn this activity from a simple improvisation drama into a full historical role-play, asking children to dress appropriately, moving the location to a local hall and asking other adults to adopt the various adult roles. This kind of elaborate enactment, although valuable, is not necessary and the power of the imagination and of symbol in drama can be just as effective, perhaps more so since it is easier to employ a range of drama strategies and to move freely in and out of role if the set up is less complex.

A key to creating this drama is the sense of ritual, of not being in control, of one's fate being decided in a way that is not clear and by rules which are not obvious.

Begin by asking the children to all become evacuees, some on their own, some in family groups of two, three, four or five. Each child will need to make a luggage label to wear on their wrist with their first name and 'family name' written on.

Make sure that the children understand the situation and, in particular, the need to do exactly what the supervisor tells them to do.

Within the drama the role of the supervisor is an important one. You could adopt the role yourself, but it may be better in this case to ask someone else to do so, allowing you to remain outside the drama, facilitating. If a parent, a student teacher or helper could be persuaded to take the role, this would help enormously.

The supervisor is strict and appears unfeeling, which is a simple device to heighten the children's sense of the kind of dislocation and uncertainty that the evacuees must have experienced.

There is a danger here that, because of the authoritative nature of the supervisor role, the children may respond negatively within the drama, taking the opportunity to challenge the supervisor and react in an unrealistic way. If this does happen, stop the drama to re-focus and talk through the reasons why this approach is inappropriate.

The drama starts when the children file into the village hall to be met by the supervisor who immediately makes clear the kind of behaviour expected of them. The children are lined up and inspected. The supervisor looks at every name tag, makes comments on scruffy writing or appearance, and then delivers a lecture about how lucky these children are and how generous their hosts are.

You can freeze the action at any point during this to allow children to speak their thoughts, using these to contrast with the strict formality of the supervisor.

One by one the children's names are called and they are removed from the lines. At this point, those children who have been called must step out of the drama for a while (unless you are able to lay on lots of adults to take them off!). They can simply sit down to watch the rest of the activity, which should now move fairly quickly until there are just a few children left.

This is one large family who don't want to be split up. There is space, the supervisor explains, for them to go to two families but no single family can take all the children together. The dilemma facing these children is whether to give in and allow themselves to be split up, or to stand their ground and refuse to budge unless they all go together.

An effective way to explore this dilemma is to use 'Conscience Alley'.

◆ *Tips for . . .* **Conscience Alley**

This is a simple technique where the class form two lines facing each other in order that those having to make the decision can walk slowly between the two lines. As they pass, each individual offers them advice, speaking as their conscience:

> You know you ought to split up, you're just causing trouble
> Just say yes or you'll be stuck here forever
> You can't let them split up the family
> It's just not fair

Having walked through the alley, the children give their response based on what they have heard.

Conscience Alley can be re-run, allowing the class to discuss what they will say and to explore the arguments before running it again. This might help to avoid the situation where all the class think that the children should simply refuse to be split up.

In order to enact the actual moment when the children tell the supervisor their decision and how the situation is resolved, you could employ Forum Theatre (see page 139).

ACTIVITY 4 **Incidents**   SMALL GROUP PLAYMAKING

WHERE? In drama space as before.

HOW? Once children have a clear grasp of evacuation and of the difficulties and issues involved, you could ask them to depict some kind of incident in a small group play. This is the kind of drama which most teachers are used to when children are asked to prepare a scene or number of scenes, to share with the rest of the class.

As a strategy it allows children a good deal of freedom in how they organise their groups, how they choose their roles and incident and how they portray it.

There are, however, inherent weaknesses in the strategy:

■ It can easily lose focus.

■ The organisational tasks (arguing over who does what) can take over from the theme.

■ Some children can tend to dominate decision making and role-playing.

Handled carefully these difficulties can be turned to opportunities, as children learn to negotiate and work together, to plan effectively and to use time intelligently.

In addition you can encourage children to think about using the full range of drama forms that they have become used to – using mime, speaking thoughts, sound pictures, etc – to allow all children to contribute in their own way.

Let them choose their own incidents. You might suggest possibilities such as:

■ the first meeting with the host family

■ making friends with the village children

■ first day at the village school

■ trying to run away.

Development across Key Stages 1 and 2 . . .

IN HISTORY The same approaches can be used in investigating incidents within other History study units in Key Stage 2.

■ **Victorian Britain** A child drafted into domestic service some way from home, or a pauper apprentice working in a cotton mill, have obvious parallels in terms of separation, change and difference, reactions to authority, social and emotional adjustments.

■ **Romans, Anglo-Saxons and Vikings in Britain** Each successive wave of invasion and settlement in Britain resulted in its own experiences of dislocation for both families and for individuals. A similar scenario could be constructed around the experience of Roman or Viking families who come to Britain, or of indigenous families who move as a result of the arrival of settlers.

IN GEOGRAPHY Similarly, the experiences of people moving from the country to a shanty town in a growing city in the developing world, or of indigenous people 'moved on' by new developments in their locality such as lumbering, mining or the building of a dam, could create fertile ground for dramatic activities.

Design a Playground SURVEYING, MAKING A PRESENTATION

Curriculum context

In these activities the children investigate their fellow pupils' attitudes to their playground space. There are obvious opportunities for developing this into a major design and technology activity. There are also plentiful opportunities to develop children's mathematical skills both in planning the sample, and in recording the results of the survey.

Key Strategies

In the first part of the activity children will be working in small groups to plan a research project into what others think of the school's playground space. They will think about possible improvements.

In the latter part they will be working with their small group to present the conclusions of their research to an audience of their classmates.

Expected outcomes

■ improved skills in small group discussion and decision making

■ improved interviewing skills

■ opportunities for presenting material using a variety of media linked by clear and succinct speech.

How to use the material

The four activities would spread well over a period of up to three weeks since each activity yields distinct and tangible results which can be returned to and looked at afresh after a short period away from the project.

All of the activities will require the children to develop good working relationships in small groups.

You will need

■ copies of the sample questionnaire and running order.

ACTIVITY 1 Preparing the playground survey
SMALL GROUP DISCUSSION

WHERE? In groups around tables.

HOW? Set the class the task of finding out what the school (as a whole) thinks of the playground provision.

Split the class into small groups – probably groups of four would be ideal. Each group will devise their own questionnaire to elicit the information. This should be an 'oral' questionnaire – that is, it prompts the interviewer to ask the questions and the interviewer fills in the respondents' answers as they reply.

Give guidance as to the areas of questioning that will be covered:

■ the size and position of the playground

■ any equipment that is provided

■ any rules which apply

■ how the playground compares with those of other schools

■ any improvements that the respondents would like to see.

The groups will also need to think about the design of the questionnaire, so that it is easy to use in the 'interview' situation.

■ Will it have simple tick boxes?

■ Will there be spaces to write in answers?

■ Will the answers to certain questions lead on to different questions? For example, 'If the answer is YES, go on to Question 3. If the answer is NO, go on to Question 5.

■ Will it include illustrations that can be shown to the respondents? For example, 'Look at this diagram of the playground. Which area do you think is the least used?'

Encourage the groups to think carefully about the questions and the most appropriate format for the response in each case.

A sample questionnaire is shown on Resource Sheet 16. This can be photocopied and used as an example.

Once the overall scope of the questionnaire is defined, the small group should assign separate tasks to individuals within the group. One child could design each page of the questionnaire, one could draw the playground plan, etc.

Each group should produce a fair copy of the questionnaire which can be photocopied so that, in every group, each child has enough questionnaires to enable them to interview their quota of respondents.

The exact number of respondents required will be determined by the time available and the practical considerations rather than statistical necessity. However, if each child in a group of four interviewed five children, that would give twenty replies which is probably enough for the group to process and use for their presentation.

If appropriate you could use this as an opportunity to discuss the notion of representative samples, perhaps relating this to the notion of a 'fair test' which the children will have come across in Science.

Resource 16

Playground Questionnaire

1. Age ....Boy ☐ Girl ☐

2. Which part of the playground do you use most often?

Ball play area ☐

Apparatus ☐

Quiet games and talk area ☐

(Show playground map when you ask this question)

3. Why do you use this area most often?

4. How could the area be improved?

5. Do you know about any other school playgrounds?

(If no, go on to question 6)

Yes ☐

No ☐

6. Is there anything which those other schools have that you would like to have here?

ACTIVITY 2 **Conducting the survey**

WHERE?   Visiting other classrooms by arrangement or in the playground at break/lunch time.

HOW?   This is a Speaking and Listening task in a real situation, needing specific skills and preparation. It will work in a similar way to a survey conducted by a company in any High Street or shopping centre.

You could require the children to make their own contact with other class teachers, perhaps by letter, in advance of the survey being conducted. If so, they will need to think about:

■ When would be an appropriate time

■ How long the survey would take

■ How they would briefly and succinctly explain the nature of the survey and its aims.

In conducting the actual survey, the groups would need to think about:

■ Whether they will work singly, in pairs or larger groups. You may want to decide this yourself – the most effective method is to work in pairs with one asking the question and the other writing down answers. The pairs can swap tasks.

■ Whether they will need a checklist before starting (copies of questionnaire, pens, etc).

■ How they will approach individuals, and on what basis they will choose the respondents.

■ What they will say by way of introduction.

As this is a 'for real' situation, the interviewers will soon learn whether they are speaking clearly and listening carefully to the responses!

ACTIVITY 3 Sharing the results

WHERE?   Back in the classroom.

HOW?   Important Speaking and Listening skills will be needed as each group finds the most appropriate way of telling the rest of the class what they have discovered.

First of all each group will need to analyse the results of their survey. How far you choose to develop the mathematical potential of this exercise will be determined by your other curriculum objectives. Comparisons could be drawn between replies according to age and gender.

Pupils will need to think about the following questions:

■ What are their main findings?

■ Which findings will be of most interest to their audience?

■ What is the clearest, most succinct way of explaining these?

■ How will they back these up with evidence?

■ Who will say what?

Each group should prepare a two-minute presentation summarising one of their main findings; for example, which area of the playground people use the most.

In their simple presentation they should include:

■ the questions they asked

■ a summary of the replies they received

■ a statement about the most-used and the least-used area

■ pointers to how the most- and least-used areas could each be improved.

Each group should practise before they present their findings to the class.

ACTIVITY 4 **The ideal playground**

WHERE? In the classroom or hall for the actual presentation, with some preparatory work at tables.

HOW? This is a longer, Design and Technology based project which builds on the results of the survey.

In groups, children design their own ideal playground then create a presentation which 'sells' the idea to the rest of the class.

In the presentation a variety of media can be used:

■ Specially taken photographs (or slides would be better for a presentation), showing features from nearby playgrounds – 'We'd like a climbing frame like this one at the Heath.'

■ Tape recordings of other children: 'We asked Mrs Patel's class what they would like to see in our playground. This is what Joseph said . . . '

■ Drawings, models and plans.

■ 'Before' and 'After' still pictures – showing children's changing attitude to the playground before and after improvements.

Groups would probably need several sessions in which to prepare for such a presentation.

A good way to keep them focused on the task over a protracted period is to ask each group to produce a script/running order so that tasks can be ticked off when completed. This will also ensure that the project retains a clear, overall shape. A sample running order is shown on page 172.

You can also give a time limit, say three minutes per group, in order to maintain a tight focus for the task.

Such a task would be given extra potency if, as in some schools, there really is an opportunity for the playground to be redeveloped taking account of children's perceptions and feelings about play-space. If so, how children would like to see their play-spaces developed would need to be set in a framework of realistic possibilities, although these may be worked out from idealistic wishes.

Sample running order/script

SIOBHAN   When we asked most people what they thought of our playground, this is what they said.

WHOLE GROUP   Terrible, yuck, rubbish, etc.

SIOBHAN   So we decided to get our own ideas for how it could be improved. Here's Mahinda to tell you how we started.

MAHINDA   *Points to result of group brainstorm on the wall and goes through some of the ideas.*

SIOBHAN   Now we're going to show you the models we made. We each took our favourite idea and tried to show what it would look like. Francis is first.

     Francis, Clare, Mahinda and Siobhan each show models and talk about them.

SIOBHAN   Now before we go any further – this is the sort of thing that happens in our playground at the moment:

     The rest of the group act out a playground argument that turns into a fight.

SIOBHAN   Freeze! (*the fight stops*). There's nothing to do, so fights happen, but if we built our new playground . . .

     The rest of the group mime happy children playing on the climbing frame etc.

SIOBHAN   So . . .

ALL   Don't muck around. Build our playground!

Development across Key Stages 1 and 2 . . .

OTHER SURVEYS   One theme of the Geography curriculum in Key Stages 1 and 2 is 'environmental quality'. The questionnaire technique can be used to help pupils to find out the views of children, staff, other adults or businesses in the community, on the quality of the environment in their own area.

The same template can apply in which children design a questionnaire, analyse results and present them to others in as engaging a way as possible.

Pupils can use survey and presentation to investigate other aspects of the school environment such as display areas, decoration, nature area etc.

OTHER PRESENTATIONS   Wherever children have to present the conclusions of a class project to others they can be encouraged to think in advance about the needs of their audience, about gearing the presentation to the audience, and increasing the impact of their presentation by careful preparation and selective use of visual aids and strategies such as we have suggested for Activity 4.

On Air – Radio News COMPOSITE

Curriculum context

These activities are English-based, investigating in particular the language requirements of sound broadcast. This will have an important place in Media studies – which, whilst not a National Curriculum subject in its own right, is an important aspect of English and language education. There are also particularly strong links to Geography (in the weather report) and Technology (in the use of the computer and the recording equipment).

Key Strategy

In these activities children make their own 'radio news' programme. They use the well-known techniques of sound broadcast such as the news report, the specialist interview and the weather forecast.

Working in groups they will need to use all the skills of group discussion. Working on the individual parts of the broadcast they will engage in interviewing, script writing and performing.

To present their programmes they will need to use their communication skills – clear and fluent speech and precise vocabulary – to get their point across.

When listening to the groups' broadcasts they will need to evaluate their own and others' talk, and to identify the important skills required for the different components of the sound broadcast.

The children will become aware of the issue of Standard English: a news broadcast requires a certain register and style of language. The choice of words is important, as is clear delivery and an approach acceptable to all listeners. These activities provide an opportunity to explore such formal and less colloquial uses of language.

Expected outcomes

■ increased understanding of presentational techniques

■ increased confidence in creative small-group work

■ increased confidence in preparing spoken language and in addressing a large group.

How to use the material

These activities build on skills already developed in earlier activities. In particular we assume that children will have done some work on interview techniques, and have used a tape recorder (see page 121 for example).

These activities could form a half or a whole day's intensive work. It would be possible to include other elements such as designing logos for the 'news teams' and perhaps a visit from a local radio reporter, etc.

The length of the finished programme is not too important, but we advise working towards a short two-minute slot in the first instance. News reporters calculate length on an average of fifteen words per five seconds, so a two-minute bulletin would still need 270 written words – assuming that 30 seconds of the bulletin is given over to an unscripted interview.

As the task is complex, we offer alternative, simpler, approaches in each of the activities. There are also four resource sheets – a planning sheet for use in Activity 1, a sample running order applicable to Activity 3, a sample script and Notes for News Teams.

You will need

■ copies of the news story plan on page 178.

ACTIVITY 1 Newsroom conference
SMALL GROUP WORK

WHERE? In groups around tables and with access to the day's newspapers.

HOW? You've set the deadline and the groups have been chosen.

The first job is for each group or 'News team' to begin to rough out the shape of their two-minute bulletin.

Give them clear parameters. We suggest that each bulletin should include at least one component from each of these categories:

■ a national story

■ a school (or local) story

■ an interview

■ a weather forecast.

You might choose to give clear guidance about the national story – choosing something where the children will not get too bogged down in complex detail. It may also be helpful to distribute copies of the planning sheet (page 178) at this stage.

Encourage the groups to think about the overall balance of the bulletin so that they avoid, for example, a bulletin entirely made up of sports stories. They will also need to consider balance in terms of tone – is it all too serious, can they find a light-hearted piece to end on?

You could listen to BBC Schools Radio's *In the News* by way of preparation. It will help them appreciate the need for balance and will highlight the distinctive style of the medium.

The news teams' next job will be to split up the elements of the programme between the group members and to agree on the research tasks.

For example, in a group of four the tasks might be split as follows:

■ Mahinda is to ask the school secretary to be interviewed about the new office computer.

■ Jamie is to research the weather and to find the most popular (broadcastable!) joke in a parallel class.

■ Thomas is to get the facts about the national story by reading the newspaper reports.

■ Rachel is to look through the local paper for a story.

A simpler alternative is for each group to prepare just one part of a whole class bulletin, so that one group works on a national story, another on a local story, a third on the weather forecast and so on.

ACTIVITY 2 **Research**

WHERE? In various locations appropriate to the story being researched.

HOW? The news teams now undertake their research. Exactly how long this takes and how it is undertaken will vary depending on how ambitious you want them to be.

Keep the approaching deadline in the children's minds by reminding them that at a specified time (not too far ahead) they will hold their last Newsroom conference before the broadcast and must be ready with their researched stories by then.

THE INTERVIEW Encourage the reporter to have questions ready in advance of any interview/research.

There are two options as to how to conduct the interview: they can research (and take notes) in order to prepare for a 'live' interview later; or they can tape-record an interview to play during the broadcast.

We favour the live interview wherever possible because of the complications of editing or cueing up a taped interview. Audio tape editing can be an instructive and enjoyable experience, but it would probably overcomplicate the present activity.

THE NATIONAL STORY AND THE LOCAL STORY Aim for a 15-second – or 45-word – summary of the story.

Aim to include a quote from someone involved in the story as well as the bare-bones of what happened. The quote can be read from a newspaper or possibly taped from a radio broadcast (but see the reservations about tape recording above).

THE WEATHER FORECAST This could be taken from the national or local newspapers, but it would be more telling if it could be based on local data – particuarly if the school has invested in one of the computer-based weather satellite systems, or simply operates its own weather station.

ACTIVITY 3 Planning the broadcast SMALL GROUP WORK

WHERE? Back in the classroom in groups around tables.

HOW? Now comes the task of reviewing the research and putting the broadcast together. Different groups will have a variety of ways of working and varying degrees of sophistication as they approach this task. The following is a guide to one method of structuring this section within each group:

- Take it in turns to hear what everyone has to say about their reporting.

- Decide together on which stories you will include and give them rough timings to make a complete bulletin of about two minutes.

- Write a 'running order' together (see sample on page 179).

- Decide which items need full scripting and which can be improvised. Typically links and stories will need scripts, interviews and some firsthand reporting can be improvised from notes.

- Allow time for writing scripts/preparing notes.

- Rehearse your bulletin at least twice.

If you are following the option of having each group rehearse only one story, you can take a more active role in this section, running a number of rehearsals and giving tips for improvements.

ACTIVITY 4 Broadcast SMALL GROUP PRESENTATION

WHERE? In the classroom, with tables at the front from which each team delivers its broadcast.

◆ *Tips for* . . . news bulletins

One of the problems with this type of work is that children's aptitude, enjoyment, and performance abilities vary so greatly and that these differences can be painfully obvious.

There are a number of ways of supporting those who find this kind of activity difficult:

- The news teams can deliver their bulletin from where they are sitting while everyone listens with their eyes closed. This takes the visual focus away from the 'performers', which may help.

- Stress what is said, rather than how it is said as such encouragement is bound to improve the 'how it is said' next time.

- Strike a balance between the 'Live News' aspect, which will foster a sense of urgency and heighten the dramatic elements, and the fact that this is a classroom exercise. It doesn't really matter if groups have to re-start their bulletin, you could stress that this type of 're-take' is the norm in broadcasting.

- Make it an enjoyable experience by 'going with' any humour (intentional or otherwise!) which develops.

- For those who really do find any speaking in front of others painful, develop other roles, such as timekeeper (with a stopwatch) or 'Director' who gives a visual cue for each item in the bulletin.

Alternative: If the whole class is delivering one bulletin you may want to think about alternative ways to create a sense of audience, of someone to broadcast to. You could require a final 'live' broadcast in which you do not participate, but simply listen. Another possibility is to tape record this version so that it can be played back to the class, or you could perform the news to another class or even the whole school in an assembly.

Development across Key Stages 1 and 2 . . .

Clearly the format of the radio news bulletin can be developed so that the programme includes a Science story (some recent research or discovery – there is usually one to be found in the news in any given week), an historical story (using for example the interviews suggested on page 122), an RE story (about a forthcoming or recent religious festival).

Resource 17

Planning Sheet

REPORTING TEAM:

Story Covered by
National

Local

Interview

Weather

Others

Sample Running Order

School News Bulletin

Running Order

No.	Story	Reporter	Duration
1.	Menu ('In today's programme . . . ')	Rachel	00.25"
2.	New Dinosaur fossil found	Thomas	00.15"
3.	Local Hockey team wins championship	Rachel	00.15"
4.	New computer arrives in school office (interview)	Mahinda	00.30"
5.	Joke survey	Jim, with jokes read by members of the team	00.25"
6.	Weather and close	Jim	00.10"

Resource 19

Sample page of script

Rachel   *Hello and welcome to Class Six News on Thursday, November the 17th. All the News that's happening in our school, our town and around the country. In today's programme:*

A new type of dinosaur has been discovered in America.

Why our town's hockey team is celebrating.

Our school has a new computer – why you won't get to use it.

The results of our joke survey.

And the weather for the rest of today.

Now, to tell us about that new dinosaur, here's Thomas Fisher.

Thomas   *The remains of a type of dinosaur never found before have been discovered in America. It's said to be a ferocious meat eater similar to T Rex but with a powerful club tail. Scientists haven't named it yet, but one local person said it should be named after our Head Teacher.*

Rachel   *Local hockey team, the Lions, will be packing their bags tonight, ready for a trip to Gibraltar tomorrow. They've won the trip by beating twenty other British teams over the past year. They'll be playing six games in Gibraltar and will be home again in a week's time.*

Mahinda   *Now, to find out why the school has a new computer but you can't use it, I'm joined by Mrs Lindridge.*

Mrs Lindridge, why do you as School Secretary need a new computer . . . ?

TIPS FOR NEWS TEAMS

Do . . .
- Make a careful plan of your bulletin.
- Work out who will do what.
- Set clear deadline times.
- Aim for a balanced broadcast with local/national items and a mix of humorous and serious stories.
- Rehearse as much as you can.

Don't . . .
- Leave everything until the last minute!
- Try to cover too many stories.
- Be too ambitious (like trying to interview the Prime Minister on Concorde about your swimming club).
- Trust that 'it'll be alright on the night' – it won't unless you plan and rehearse.

When interviewing:
- Have a clear idea of why you are interviewing this person – what do you want to get out of them?
- Be polite but try to make them answer *your* question.
- Have plenty of questions prepared in advance.
- Be ready to depart from your planned questions if something more interesting is said.
- Always carry a note book and pencil.

When interviewing:
- Don't interview someone until you've done your research and you know the exact area you want to cover and have your first couple of questions ready.
- Don't let the person you're interviewing wander off the subject.
- Don't be rude.
- Don't keep asking the same question if you think you've heard all the person has to say.

When writing your script:
- Write it for you to *speak*. Keep practising every few seconds to hear how it sounds and how easy it is to read out loud.
- Remember the length you've been given and remember 15 words take about 5 seconds.

When writing your script:
- Don't put in unnecessary words, keep it clear and simple.
- Don't read straight from your first notes, always make a fair copy (either hand written or using a word processor).

Using BBC Radio Drama, Stories and Poetry

In this section we explore the potential of the BBC Schools' radio output to provide engaging and stimulating listening, leading to quality follow up work by pupils.

For some teachers, using programmes of this kind can feel like a 'cop out', as if the teacher is relying on someone else's preparation and ideas. It is central to our approach that these resources should be teacher mediated, and treated as flexible materials to be used much as one might use a piece of prose, a poem, a picture or a music stimulus.

Interactive drama programmes

These offer a story, usually linked to a specific curriculum area, which the class are invited to explore by taking on various roles. The engaging storylines are designed to involve the children – the story-teller is often in role as part of the drama.

At the time of writing there are two series for Key Stage 2: *First Steps in Drama*, for the 7–9 age group, and *Drama Workshop* for 9–12-year-olds (this series is also popular in the early years of secondary school). For Key Stage 1 the interactive drama series is *Let's Make a Story*.

By way of example, the series have recently explored subjects and curriculum areas as diverse as:

- the Romans, Saxons, Ancient Egyptians, Ancient Greece
- ecology and green issues
- George Stephenson and the building of the railways
- the life of a Victorian servant
- a ghost story
- The Tower of London/The Fire of London
- A journey to the Earth's core
- life in the shadow of a volcano
- *Fungus the Bogeyman*
- African legends and stories
- Diwali/Christmas.

In each case a story is told by a 'Narrator' and through dramatised scenes.

The 'Narrator' also sets up drama activities (about six per programme) which the children and teacher undertake, usually switching off a tape of the broadcast to allow flexible time for the drama.

The programmes develop children's listening skills by requiring them to:

■ follow a story told by a narrator

■ understand and distil information from dramatised scenes using all the conventions of radio drama

■ listen to instructions and act on them

■ respond through movement (and sometimes talk in role as well) to sound effect sequences.

These skills are developed through the 'hook' of an engaging story and, where the programmes work well, children respond enthusiastically to the material and develop their listening abilities alongside their enjoyment of the drama.

It is not our intention here to cover individual series or programmes, but rather to look at strategies for using these broadcasts.

The drama activities for each programme are fully explored in the Teachers' Notes which accompany each series.

FOLLOWING A WHOLE PROGRAMME

This is the most common method of using the broadcasts. The programmes are taped off air and then used with the whole class, usually in the hall. The following 'Golden Rules' will help teachers get the most out of the material:

■ **Be selective**   Using the BBC Annual Programme (a booklet sent free to every school), and the Teachers' Notes (which can be ordered from the Annual Programme), record those broadcasts which will fit into your curriculum work for a given term (the programmes must be tape recorded; the interactive nature means they will not work 'off air'). This allows you to take time over those specific programmes to broaden the children's knowledge and involvement. If, for example, you are exploring the world of the Tudors, a unit of *Drama Workshop* set in that period will draw on knowledge that the children already possess, and will help to flesh out their more academic work through the engagement of drama.

There may well be other units which you wish to use because they develop specific drama or listening skills, all of which will be useful when you come to programmes related to particular curriculum areas.

■ **Listen in advance**   If time allows, listen to the programmes before using them so that you can anticipate any areas of concern or elements that will need further clarification or explanation for your pupils.

■ **Plan your own involvement**   Many activities will be enhanced if you adopt a simple role while the children work:

– a sceptical villager, challenging the class's view on a particular matter

– a fellow worker, digging the canal alongside everyone else

– a photographer, looking at each 'Still Picture' in turn, as if it is a photograph you are taking.

None of the above need involve you in dramatic or solo 'performances'!

In terms of structured listening, your role can be to check the information the children should have before allowing them to move on to the task. You can do this as yourself or in role: 'So villagers, let's just remind ourselves of the crime Annie is supposed to have committed before deciding what to do with her. Who can tell me what happened?'

You also have the option of replaying a particular scene or section of narration.

There will also be occasions when you will need to give pointers to what the children need to listen out for as they return to listening – perhaps a mystery will be solved or they will gain clues to what has happened.

■ **Provide additional structure**   As in most areas of education, the children's listening will be enhanced if they are clear about what is expected of them. Many teachers develop a few simple rules which enhance the listening, and thus the drama, experience.

– Even when asked to do something by the Narrator, the children should wait for a signal from the teacher before moving.

– Always listen in silence but a child may raise his or her hand if there's anything he or she doesn't understand.

– As soon as an activity is over, we all return to sit by the tape recorder, ready for the next section of listening.

USING SELECTED SCENES   One difficulty of using these programmes is that whatever the children decide about a specific question or issue in their own drama, as soon as the tape is switched on again it follows a predetermined course which may conflict with where the class want to take the drama!

The programmes use a number of devices to get around these problems and to allow the children genuine choices, but if they do not suit your needs it is still possible to use any given scene as a starting point and then to switch off the tape and let the drama follow its own course.

■ Choose your scene! An obvious starting point and one which will require you to listen to at least part of the tape before working with the class. The beginning of the story is often the first choice, but it may be that you prefer to start a little later on, when an exciting point or climax is reached, filling in the story so far yourself. To develop listening skills, choose a scene which gives plenty of background information and switch off the tape before the narrator interjects. You can then question the class on what they have picked up from listening before moving on to set up a drama activity.

In terms of drama, you will get the most immediate response if, in the scene you use, there is a dilemma involved, or if some other tension is present. For example, a scene where animal rights protestors outside a zoo are trying to prevent people entering, as in the *Drama Workshop* production 'Here is the News'.

■ Develop your drama skills. Although many teachers would feel unhappy about developing a drama session in so free a manner, one of the strengths of the programmes is that as they use them, teacher and class learn a range of techniques and approaches to drama which they can apply to different situations. So here's a listening task for the teacher! Listen to the programme at home or in the car and take particular note of how the drama activities are set up and used.

■ Use the broadcast to give you options. If you can find time to listen to the whole tape, then you will at least have a structure in mind which you can follow, and a number of activities which can be developed should you need ideas to feed in. The teachers' notes will also be a useful source of ideas.

Stories and poetry programmes

There is a wealth of story and poetry output for use in schools. As well as specific School Radio programmes, there are dramatisations on Radio 4 and a number of cassettes are available commercially. There is also audio material on a growing number of interactive CDs.

It is a good idea to get into the habit of recording a number of radio programmes. Apart from the cost of the tape and the capital cost of the recording equipment, the actual programmes are free and copies can be used many times. Details of programmes are available in the *Radio Times* and, with much more information, in the *BBC Schools Annual Programme*. The following are some suggestions for getting the most out of these audio resources.

■ **Equipment** Do aim for good quality equipment with sufficient clarity and volume on playback and a good quality tuner section for recording. There are specialist manufacturers who produce cassette recorders especially for schools. It is also possible to have a built-in timer so that programmes can be recorded automatically. Alternatively, with some equipment an external timer, sold in high street shops, can be used.

■ **Library** Keep an indexed library of recordings. It is possible to save a small amount of money by recording on the same tape every week, thus wiping last week's programme, but this is a false economy. If you keep the tapes, and know where to find an individual programme, they'll prove a valuable teaching resource that can be used over and over again. A parent who is not free to help in school might be able to record and index the tapes at home for you.

■ **Listening groups** Perhaps the most common way to use stories and poems is in class groups. The advantages of this in terms of organisation are clear, as is the fact that the whole class can then discuss the material and undertake follow up work on it. However, there are other ways of using tapes:

– A listening post with a simple tape-recorder and up to four sets of headphones can enable individual or small group listening without disturbing the rest of the class. Again, such equipment is available from specialist manufacturers. One way of organising this is simply to require each child to have listened to a particular story or collection of poems at some point during the week – you could have a tick list for each child to indicate that they have listened. The 'follow on' work could be equally staggered, perhaps with a time of sharing on Friday afternoon.

– If you have the staff and space, a helper could take small groups out to listen. Small groups are particularly useful for assessing the children's understanding and input into discussions.

– Very occasionally, you may want to bring the whole school together to hear a poem or short story – indeed this happens every week with the popular assembly series, 'Together'.

■ **Join in!** Many programmes have opportunies for children to send in material which may be used on air. The poetry programmes often end the term with listeners' own poems and other programmes feature children's letters and comments. *In the News*, the weekly radio news programme for children, is a good example. This can be a most effective way of stimulating writing and can give an extra edge to the children's listening.

■ **DIY!** Once children have become used to listening to programmes, and have a feel for the way they are constructed, they can try making their own:

– A news programme with children reporting on events at school and news of the local community (see 'Newsroom Conference', page 174). This could be sent to children at a neighbouring school, played to parents, even offered to a local or hospital radio station.

– A drama/story programme with carefully rehearsed sound effects. This could be played to parallel or younger classes, or perhaps be used in an assembly.

– A poetry compilation where a small group record their poems in sequence (perhaps with linking material and/or music) as an alternative to reading them out loud to the class. Bilingual children could record a poem/prayer etc. in their mother tongue for others to listen to.

Such compilations could be available at the listening post or set up in a foyer area so that visitors have something to listen to as they wait.

For information about BBC School programmes you can refer to *Radio Times*, the *BBC Schools Annual Programme* (sent free to every school) or telephone the Education Information Hotline on 0181 746 1111.